Cambridge Elements

Elements in Experimental Political Science
edited by
James N. Druckman
University of Rochester

THE POWER OF THE CROWD

How the Public Can Both Spoil and Improve Social Media as a Source of Information

Florian Stöckel
University of Exeter

Sabrina Stöckli
Bern University of Applied Sciences

Benjamin A. Lyons
University of Utah

Hannah Kroker
University of Edinburgh

Jason Reifler
University of Southampton

Shaftesbury Road, Cambridge CB2 8EA, United Kingdom

One Liberty Plaza, 20th Floor, New York, NY 10006, USA

477 Williamstown Road, Port Melbourne, VIC 3207, Australia

314–321, 3rd Floor, Plot 3, Splendor Forum, Jasola District Centre, New Delhi – 110025, India

103 Penang Road, #05–06/07, Visioncrest Commercial, Singapore 238467

Cambridge University Press is part of Cambridge University Press & Assessment, a department of the University of Cambridge.

We share the University's mission to contribute to society through the pursuit of education, learning and research at the highest international levels of excellence.

www.cambridge.org
Information on this title: www.cambridge.org/9781009677134
DOI: 10.1017/9781009677165

© Florian Stöckel, Sabrina Stöckli, Benjamin A. Lyons, Hannah Kroker and Jason Reifler 2025

This work is in copyright. It is subject to statutory exceptions and to the provisions of relevant licensing agreements; with the exception of the Creative Commons version the link for which is provided below, no reproduction of any part of this work may take place without the written permission of Cambridge University Press.

An online version of this work is published at doi.org/10.1017/9781009677165 under a Creative Commons Open Access licence CC-BY-NC-ND 4.0 which permits re-use, distribution and reproduction in any medium for non-commercial purposes providing appropriate credit to the original work is given. You may not distribute derivative works without permission. To view a copy of this licence, visit https://creativecommons.org/licenses/by-nc-nd/4.0

All versions of this work may contain content reproduced under license from third parties. Permission to reproduce this third-party content must be obtained from these third-parties directly.

When citing this work, please include a reference to the DOI 10.1017/9781009677165

First published 2025

A catalogue record for this publication is available from the British Library

ISBN 978-1-009-67717-2 Hardback
ISBN 978-1-009-67713-4 Paperback
ISSN 2633-3368 (online)
ISSN 2633-335X (print)

Additional resources for this publication at www.cambridge.org/stoeckel.

Cambridge University Press & Assessment has no responsibility for the persistence or accuracy of URLs for external or third-party internet websites referred to in this publication and does not guarantee that any content on such websites is, or will remain, accurate or appropriate.

For EU product safety concerns, contact us at Calle de José Abascal, 56, 1°, 28003 Madrid, Spain, or email eugpsr@cambridge.org

The Power of the Crowd

How the Public Can Both Spoil and Improve Social Media as a Source of Information

Elements in Experimental Political Science

DOI: 10.1017/9781009677165
First published online: September 2025

Florian Stöckel
University of Exeter

Sabrina Stöckli
Bern University of Applied Sciences

Benjamin A. Lyons
University of Utah

Hannah Kroker
University of Edinburgh

Jason Reifler
University of Southampton

Author for correspondence: Florian Stöckel, f.stoeckel@exeter.ac.uk

Abstract: This Element explores misinformation as a challenge for democracies, using experiments from Germany, Italy, and the UK to assess the role of user-generated corrections on social media. A sample of more than 170,000 observations across a wide range of topics (COVID, climate change, 5G, etc.) is used to test whether social corrections help reduce the perceived accuracy of false news and whether miscorrections decrease the credibility of true news. Corrections reduce the perceived accuracy of misinformation, but miscorrections can harm perceptions of true news. The Element also assesses the mechanisms of social corrections, finding evidence for recency effects rather than systematic processing. Additional analyses show the characteristics of individuals who have more difficulties identifying false news. Survey data is included on characteristics of people who write comments often. The conclusion highlights that social corrections can mislead but also work as a remedy. The Element ends with best practices for effective corrections. This title is also available as open access on Cambridge Core.

Keywords: interventions, social media, misinformation, democracy, digital media literacy

© Florian Stöckel, Sabrina Stöckli, Benjamin A. Lyons, Hannah Kroker and Jason Reifler 2025

ISBNs: 9781009677172 (HB), 9781009677134 (PB), 9781009677165 (OC)
ISSNs: 2633-3368 (online), 2633-335X (print)

Contents

1 Misinformation as a Challenge for Democracy   1
2 Who Believes False News?   9
3 The Core Experimental Setup   20
4 Social Corrections, Miscorrections, and Accuracy
   Perceptions   32
5 Who Writes Comments?   52
6 Implications and Outlook   62

   References   69

1 Misinformation as a Challenge for Democracy

This section has three goals: It defines the challenge that misinformation poses, it takes stock of well-known interventions, and it situates users and user comments in this context. Thus, Section 1.1 briefly outlines the nature of the problem: What is false information and why is it a problem? False information – especially about politics – did not enter the public domain with social media, but social media changes the way it can be spread. False information is used by a variety of actors – from politicians down to voters – to hurt opponents, and it can be literally lethal; for example, when people believe false information about vaccines and do not get vaccinated.

Section 1.2 takes stock of solutions to the problem of misinformation. Scholars have already found a variety of tools that can help in the fight against misinformation: This includes accuracy prompts (Pennycook et al., 2021a, 2021b), debunking (Lewandowsky et al., 2020), prebunking or inoculation (van der Linden et al., 2017; Roozenbeek et al., 2022), and media literacy tips (Guess et al., 2020), to name some of the frequently cited interventions. We now have empirical evidence on the effectiveness of different tools and we know their limitations. For instance, debunking can lead to backfire effects (Nyhan & Reifler, 2010), although this does not seem to be the case most of the time (Swire-Thompson et al., 2020). Inoculation or literacy interventions might not reach the target audience most in need of training, since we are likely to consider ourselves better at detecting false news than we often are (Lyons et al., 2021). Many interventions are also likely to make people generally more skeptical about any information they see rather than better at discerning between what is true and what is false (Clayton et al., 2020; Modirrousta-Galian & Higham, 2023).

Section 1.3 zooms in on the role of social media users, what we know about their role in spreading misinformation online, and whether their contributions might be an intervention in their own right. Social media is a source of information for people, but people also approach it with caution (Wike et al., 2022). People also play a key role in spreading and amplifying misinformation (Guess & Lyons, 2020). However, there is now also new research which shows that user comments that correct inaccurate information on social media can help others to identify false content. Case studies come from the US and misinformation about the Zika virus (Bode & Vraga, 2018), and from India where a broader set of topics was used (Badrinathan & Chauchard, 2023). This highlights the potential that user comments have – far from being irrelevant, they can shape accuracy judgments in these (nonpartisan) cases. However, initial evidence also suggests that instances where users claim that accurate information is inaccurate affects other users (Vraga & Bode, 2022), which motivates our systematic cross-country analysis of the upsides and downsides of user corrective comments.

1.1 Definition and Examples

What is misinformation? Misinformation is false information that may be generated and spread either intentionally or unintentionally. When an actor intentionally propagates false or misleading content, this is considered disinformation – a subset of misinformation (Guess & Lyons, 2020). The question of what is "false" can undoubtedly give rise to complex epistemological concerns, though. Typically, definitions of misinformation focus on whether information contradicts expert consensus (Nyhan & Reifler, 2010; Tucker et al., 2018; Guess & Lyons, 2020). However, expertise can be contested (who counts as an expert?), and inappropriate experts can be platformed and amplified by contesting sides (Vraga & Bode, 2020). Further, there are many issues for which expert consensus is not available. According to Vraga and Bode (2020, p. 138),

> "a definition that emphasizes the "best available evidence" (Garrett, Weeks, & Neo, 2016, p. 333) may be more appropriate when expert consensus does not exist, especially further limited to information considered incorrect based on the best available evidence from relevant experts at the time. Such a definition may be more applicable to political domains for which the scientific community has not weighed in or wherein expertise is less readily established and accepted as free from bias."

Even then, evidence is subject to change – especially in fields like public health (Lyons et al., 2020). And for some questions, contradictory or speculative evidence is all there is. In such cases misinformation is "temporally bound," such that what is considered true at one point in time may shift as new evidence is gathered (Vraga & Bode, 2020). In any event, while many cases of misinformation are clear-cut and easily categorized, we must acknowledge that others are more nuanced.

Misinformation and disinformation on social media come from a range of sources – including anonymous users, influencers, alternative media, mass media, elected officials, and institutions. As such, their dissemination is driven by many goals – ideological, electoral, geopolitical, economic, and even simply chaotic (Petersen et al., 2023), as well as the purely accidental. Some forms of misinformation are more dangerous than others. Often, a particular piece of false information causes no direct harm. But in other cases, such as misinformation surrounding childhood vaccines, for instance, its effects can be harmful not only to the audience who accepts it but also to the wider community. Further, disinformation can intentionally inflame racial animus by way of "identity propaganda," or "narratives that strategically target and exploit identity-based differences in accord with pre-existing power structures to maintain hegemonic social orders" (Reddi et al., 2023, p. 2201). Likewise, misinformation may stoke anti-immigrant sentiment (Abascal et al., 2021) or be used to justify antidemocratic behaviors (as in recent events in Brazil, the US, and elsewhere) with violent consequences, particularly when it comes from the top (Rossini et al., 2023). Social media-fueled misinformation notably led to nearly two dozen people being killed by vigilante mobs in India in 2018 (Goel et al., 2018).

Even in more mundane cases, misinformation can cause voters to support candidates who are not in line with their true underlying preferences (reducing "correct voting"; Robison, 2021). Its impact on the political realm is not strictly a problem of influencing a single belief and its subsequent behavior, though. There are broader systemic effects to consider (Guess & Lyons, 2020). A constant refrain about a deluge of misinformation and public discourse surrounding its prevalence can give politicians cover for their actual intentions to deceive the public (Van Duyn & Collier, 2019; Ulusoy et al., 2021). In other words, there are cumulative effects on trust in institutions that outweigh single-case effects, given the second-order influence on a vast array of reliable information downstream.

Considering the nature of socially mediated misinformation puts additional focus on the way these platforms transform older modes of information sharing. Put simply, the combination of social media users' psychology and platform affordances can help spread misinformation in previously unseen ways and speeds. Users are frequently found within like-minded clusters, despite mixed research findings on the prevalence of echo chambers (Guess et al., 2018). These network configurations can foster the exposure and dissemination of agreeable misinformation (Del Vicario et al., 2016; Shin et al., 2017). Similarly, social media users tend to place considerable trust in their close friends. When it comes to trust in news shared on platforms like Facebook, studies indicate that the person sharing the news matters more than the news organization itself (American Press Institute, 2017). Users are more inclined to perceive news as accurate and unbiased when it is shared by someone they trust. This dynamic may contribute to the spread of misinformation, especially since platforms prioritize displaying posts from close friends to drive engagement. Consequently, algorithmic bias emerges as a result of the design choices made by most social media platforms, which prioritize engagement by favoring popular content over trustworthy information in users' feeds (Ciampaglia et al., 2018).

1.2 The State of Solutions

There are of course numerous top-down misinformation mitigation strategies that fall at the policy or platform level. Perhaps most indirectly, comparative research on media systems and Western democracies' resilience to disinformation suggest increased funding for public media can help buffer and dilute the power of propaganda and other mistruths (Humprecht et al., 2023). Political maneuvers have been initiated, such as France's legal framework that empowers judges to order the removal of "fake news." Platforms meanwhile have attempted various forms of deplatforming and demonetization of accounts spreading misleading information, but to mixed results (Ribeiro et al., 2024). At the level of individual posts, different social platforms have engaged in moderation, flagging, and debunking techniques – also to mixed results. When Twitter flagged Donald Trump's tweets about the 2020 election as false, for instance, messages with warning labels spread further than those without labels, while messages that had been blocked on Twitter remained popular on Facebook, Instagram, and Reddit (Sanderson et al., 2021). Facebook's warning labels for false stories, meanwhile, have been found to promote overly skeptical evaluations of legitimate news (Clayton et al., 2020). Efficacy aside, policy and platform level interventions also require tremendous political will to enact and may cause backlash among the public or platforms' user bases due to discomfort with censorship (Saltz et al., 2021).

At the individual level, though, a handful of promising "bottom-up" interventions have been found to reduce belief in and spread of false news stories, many of them replicated across numerous countries. Accuracy prompts – which address the problem of inattention and carelessness and simply intend to remind users that the accuracy of the information they share is important – have been found to reliably improve the public's discernment of true and false news and improve the quality of information they share in the wild (Pennycook et al., 2021b). However, these prompts likely cannot convince a reader that information they have considered at length and strongly endorse is in fact wrong.

Other researchers have studied the potential to educate or train news consumers to be more digitally literate and aware of manipulation techniques. Lateral reading encourages news consumers to act like a professional fact-checker by verifying the veracity of each story in concurrent in-depth web searches about the authors, sources, and topic. This technique has been found to improve the ability of students to assess credibility of digital content, but is relatively intensive, requiring hours if not months of training sessions (Wineburg et al., 2022). While potentially viable if integrated in school curricula, this sort of solution is more difficult to provide to broader adult populations. Brief digital literacy tips have shown promise as a scalable, low-investment approach that likewise improves discernment between true and false information (Guess et al., 2020). Though effective up to several weeks later, the effects of such tips appear to decline and would require refreshing. Lastly, researchers have developed educational games to help people spot manipulation techniques (Roozenbeek et al., 2022). While effective at reducing belief in false content, these approaches (as others) might cause a significant degree of skepticism in reliable news content (Modirrousta-Galian & Higham, 2023).

In general, many of these interventions may have significant unintended effects in causing such cynicism (Acerbi et al., 2022) and in the prioritization of "doing your own research" (Chinn & Hasell, 2023). However, "doing your own research" may simply be a proxy for anti-expert views, rather than the embrace of cautious information search. Similarly, given the rise of such sentiments globally (Lyons et al., 2021; Han et al., 2022; Spälti et al., 2023), interventions aimed at urging users to privilege authoritative mainstream media outlets and expert commentary may be ineffective among those who consume and share the highest volume of misleading content (Lyons et al., 2021). This points to the need for solutions that do not rely exclusively on authoritative sources, but rather (correct) information relayed by trusted interpersonal contacts.

1.3 Social Corrections

Social media users play a considerable role in spreading false information and dubious news stories online (Guess & Lyons, 2020). But just as crucially, average users can help temper its spread. A significant portion of social media users engage in correcting others when they come across misinformation online, actions which are visible to an even larger group (Chadwick & Vaccari, 2019; Bode & Vraga, 2021a, 2021b). When surveyed, most Americans not only expressed appreciation for these corrections, but also considered it a public responsibility (Bode & Vraga, 2021a). Such social corrections (also known as observational corrections, i.e., corrective cues placed by other social media users) have been shown to be effective at preventing the spread of health-related online misinformation (e.g., Bode & Vraga, 2018). Clearly, it is important to better understand this behavior in terms of how much good (or harm) it may cause.

Seeing others add corrective cues to a post can (1) reduce how accurate one perceives this post to be, (2) reduce the probability of interacting with this post, (3) alter one's attitudes toward the post, and (4) decrease one's intention to do what the post recommends (Bode & Vraga, 2018; Margolin et al., 2018; Colliander, 2019; Tully et al., 2020; Walter et al., 2021; Badrinathan & Chauchard, 2023). There are several favorable aspects to social corrections as a buffer against misinformation. First, such behavior is already a considerable aspect of online discussions, organically growing out of the conversational norms of online platforms. Along these lines, then, they represent a highly scalable approach to curbing the spread of misinformation. Even if a minority of social media users engage in corrective action, this represents millions of engaged social fact-checkers – free of charge. Perhaps just as importantly, social corrections also come from sources that other users, especially those with strong anti-expert sentiments or mainstream media distrust, are more likely to trust.

On the other hand, there are a number of potential drawbacks to relying on this strategy. First, there are factors working to disincentivize this behavior. Social corrections rely on individuals to act in the public good – and even then, to do so, they must first be interested in news and public affairs. Most users on social platforms do not post much about hard news and politics given preferences for entertainment and social content (Kalogeropoulos et al., 2017; Moretto et al., 2022). The social dynamics of correcting friends and family members can also be dicey, especially for younger users (Vijaykumar et al., 2022), further disincentivizing this behavior. In short, there are costs to engaging with misinformation, which can act as a barrier.

Further, important questions about the generalizability of social corrections' efficacy remain: Do these corrections work beyond the health context in the US? Does the effect of social corrections depend on their form and strength? Researchers testing the effect of social corrections have mostly focused on health topics with US samples (Bode & Vraga, 2018; Tully et al., 2020; Walter et al., 2021; for two exceptions, see Boot et al., 2021; Badrinathan & Chauchard, 2023). It is particularly important to examine whether such messages are effective for more contested topics (e.g., political news) that might trigger directional-motivated reasoning and hence rejection, as some work suggests social corrections may be more limited in these cases (Vraga et al., 2019). Second, existing research has operationalized social corrections in different ways – from subtle, standard social media reactions (e.g., like, angry emoji) to substantiated corrective comments with links to bolstering webpages that have been reposted many times (Tully et al., 2020). Hence, we do not know to what extent the form and strength of social correction measures determine their effect.

Lastly, average users are not experts. Therefore, they may unknowingly engage in *miscorrection*. Does falsely "correcting" true news items have similar but, given their veracity, less desirable effects? Vraga and Bode (2022) warn that social miscorrections of true news might amplify the spread of misinformation, at least in some cases. Specifically, they find that when social media users flag factually accurate information – for example, tick bites can trigger an allergy to red meat – as incorrect, people are less likely to believe this information. Our research is dedicated to better understanding these potential strengths and weaknesses of social corrections.

1.4 Overview of the Element

In Section 2, we map the nature of the problem by examining respondents' ability to correctly identify false and true news in social media posts in the UK, Italy, and Germany. Our analysis is based on forty-seven different posts that span a wide range of topics, drawn from actual online content. The false news posts originate from material flagged by fact-checking organizations in the respective countries. We also explore which types of news stories are particularly difficult to assess and identify the correlates of (in)correctly perceiving their veracity. Section 3 presents the experimental research design. We use a within-subjects design and conduct fieldwork in three countries, allowing us to assess the homogeneity of effects across different European contexts. In Section 4, we discuss the results: Based on experiments conducted in the UK, Italy, and Germany, we find that social corrections can help people identify false news. However, we also find that miscorrections – comments which raise doubts about true news – also affect accuracy perceptions. Miscorrections decrease the perceived accuracy of true news, even when the logo of a news outlet is displayed. In this section, we also outline potential mechanisms. Our results support the notion that user comments seem to work as (warning) signals that are processed rather superficially instead of triggering more complex reasoning. In Section 5, we use additional survey data from Germany to shed light on people's views on user comments and the characteristics of people who comment often. In Section 6, we discuss the implications. For instance, our results show that digital literacy is important not only to help people differentiate between true and false content but also to shield them from misleading comments from other users. The potential of corrective comments lies in the fact that they offer all users a way to improve the information environment on social media, even if platforms do not act. Table 1 shows an overview of key terms used in this Element.

Table 1 Key concepts and definitions

Concept	Definition
Misinformation	Misinformation is false information that may be generated and spread either intentionally or unintentionally. It contradicts expert consensus or the best available evidence on the topic.

Table 1 (cont.)

Concept	Definition
False news	A form of misinformation, this refers to *news* that contradicts expert consensus or the best available evidence on a topic. In our study, we rely on fact-checking organizations' assessments in each country to identify false news, as they debunk information and cite evidence.
True news	News supported by expert consensus or the best available evidence on a topic.
Accuracy perception	Our main outcome measure, which assesses how respondents perceive each news item. We measure this using a four-point scale with the following response categories: "not at all accurate," "not accurate," "accurate," and "very accurate."
Correction	In the context of our study, this is a user-written comment that flags a social media post containing false information as inaccurate. Corrections may include a comment with or without a link to a fact-checking source.
Miscorrection	In the context of our study, this is a user-written comment that falsely claims that an accurate social media post contains misinformation.
Source cue	A symbol, logo, or name indicating the source of a piece of information. In our study, this typically refers to the name of a newspaper, media outlet, or social media account associated with the content.
Low/high amplification	In the context of our study, this refers to the strength of the signal conveyed by a correction or miscorrection. Corrections can appear stronger when they receive more likes or when multiple corrective comments are present under a social media post. A greater number of corrective comments enhances the signal, making it more "amplified."
Ideological alignment	One contributing factor to believing misinformation is a tendency to accept claims that align with one's worldview or ideological orientation, even when the information is false. We use "ideological

Table 1 (cont.)

Concept	Definition
	alignment" to refer to whether information aligns with a person's worldview or attitudes toward a topic. Another commonly used term for this concept is congeniality.
Anti-expert sentiment	A measure assessing whether respondents view experts negatively or have greater confidence in their own expertise relative to experts. We use a common measure from the literature that combines three items, including: "I am more confident in my opinion than other people's facts" (Han et al., 2022).
Susceptibility to social influence	Measures how easily individuals adapt their behavior and attitudes based on others' actions. We use a seven-item scale (Stöckli et al., 2020) that includes items such as: "I base my decisions on information I gain from online social network posts and interactions."
Cognitive reflection	Higher cognitive reflection skills indicate a greater tendency to engage in deliberate reasoning. To measure this trait, survey respondents answer questions designed to elicit intuitive but incorrect responses. Providing the correct response requires deliberate reflection and overcoming the initial intuitive answer.

2 Who Believes False News?

As we highlight in Section 1, the key aim of our project is to understand the ways in which average citizens can affect political and scientific discourse in the face of misinformation and misleading claims shared on social media. Importantly, the data that we have collected from our experimental protocol allows us to first set important context about how people evaluate content available on social media. In so doing, we provide a unique picture of several important quantities: the extent to which people believe the false news stories in our sample and the characteristics of these users, as well as the share of people that consider the true news in our sample inaccurate and what the features of these individuals are. In broad outline, our empirical approach is simple and straightforward – we show respondents social media posts, using random assignment to allocate them, to receive different versions of our social media stimuli to examine the causal role of these variations on key outcomes. At the same time, we can use "baseline" stimuli without experimental additions to better understand to what extent people believe or do not believe true and false news, and what their characteristics are.

Consistent with other social media research, our respondents only see headlines as they would appear on platforms, and are not able to click through and read the whole article (see Neubaum & Krämer, 2017; Vraga & Bode, 2017; Colliander, 2019; Lyons et al., 2021; Epstein et al., 2023). There are, however, several reasons why focusing on headlines is a procedure that maximizes both internal and external validity. For instance, some social media platforms, like Facebook, have been optimized to show a headline, an image, and very few lines of the article (Garz & Szucs, 2023). Fifty-nine percent of links shared on Twitter are not even clicked (Gabielkov et al., 2016), and Dor (2003) shows that skilled news readers mostly use headlines rather than articles for their news consumption. Individuals have also been found to use heuristics when going through news headlines, as it is a quick way to decide which ones to read. Effortful evaluation of evidence and arguments is not how people typically engage with content. Consequently, this approach is also likely to get more directly at the problem, because users who are eager to read more before sharing an article or those who are even unwilling to rate the accuracy of information just based on a headline are not the main drivers of the prevalence of misinformation (Spezzano et al., 2021).

2.1 The Challenge of True and False News Identification on Social Media

To better understand how people evaluate and respond to social media content that contains both true and false claims, we conducted studies in three countries (UK, Italy, and Germany). In each of these countries, we use non-probability quota samples that reflect the populations with regard to age, gender, education, and region.

We generated forty-seven stimuli, all derived from social media posts that were shared on different platforms. The material was collected in the months leading up to the fieldwork: January–July 2022 for the UK, February–August 2022 for Italy, and July 2022–January 2023 for Germany. False news stories were identified through fact-checking organizations in each country, ensuring that they were sufficiently prominent to be flagged for verification. COVID-19 was particularly prevalent among the debunked materials, but our goal was to cover a broad range of topics (Clifford & Rainey, 2025). To achieve this, we included posts on several public health issues (e.g., COVID-19, vaccines, smoking), technology (e.g., the 5G cellphone network), climate change, and Russia's attack on Ukraine (see the online appendix for all details).

Different topics are likely to vary in the extent to which they trigger motivated reasoning, meaning that respondents may be more inclined to believe misinformation on some topics than others. To account for this, we measured respondents' attitudes toward the topics of the stimuli, allowing us to control for ideological alignment in the experimental analysis (a detailed presentation of the experimental research design follows in Section 3).

Although our selection of stimuli is not a representative sample, we are confident that it captures a realistic range of the types of content people encounter on social media. Our approach includes a larger number of news headlines than many comparable studies, which often focus on a single topic, a single platform, or a single country. Importantly, our design incorporates both true and false headlines (Pennycook et al., 2021a). By covering multiple topics, reflecting diverse social media platforms, and spanning three countries, our study provides broader generalizability than previous research.

The headlines reflect what has been shared on social media, but we recreated the posts with an open-source social media simulator (Zeoob.com) rather than using screenshots. This approach made it possible to randomly generate user names and faces from a photo database (Flickr-Faces-HQ Dataset, FFHQ). Moreover, by recreating the posts, we were able to control features like the number of likes and comments, which was essential for our experimental treatments.

Figure 1 shows the perceived accuracy of the various false claim headlines used in our studies. We find variation of rating headlines accurate, ranging from 18 percent (for a headline about Russia's invasion of Ukraine, see Figure 2) to 59 percent of respondents (for a headline about the greenhouse gas emissions from private jets flown to the COP26 climate summit in Glasgow, see Figure 3).

Turning next to the perceived accuracy of true news, we again see substantial variation (Figure 4). Comfortably, as a test of face validity of our stimuli, our samples rate these headlines as significantly more accurate, on average, than the headlines with false claims. The true news story that is considered accurate by the largest number of people is one about long COVID (Figure 5). Eighty-five percent of respondents consider this story to be true. The true news story that is perceived as accurate by the smallest share of respondents is regarded as misinformation by almost three out of five respondents (57 percent). It is a story about child soldiers in Ukraine (Figure 6). While only one false news story was perceived as accurate by half of the sample, four of the true news stories were not considered accurate by half the sample or more ("Saharan dust

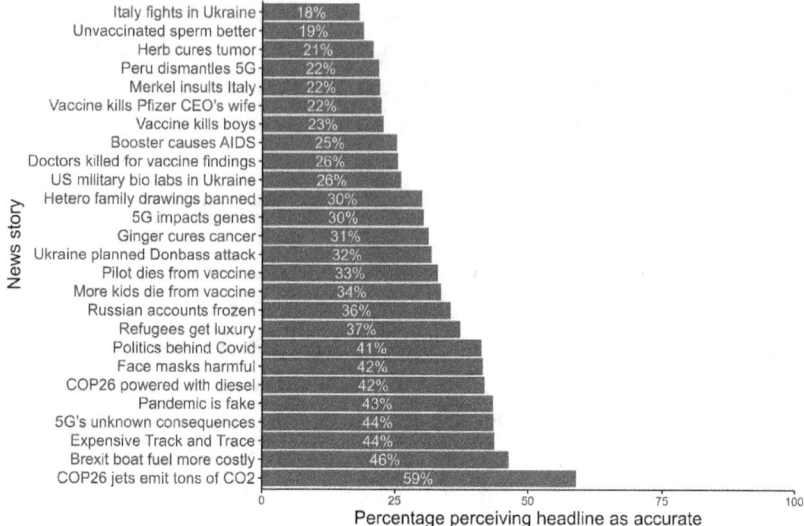

Figure 1 Percentage of false news headlines perceived as accurate or very accurate (combined share). Respondents rated all posts on a four-point scale: not at all accurate, not accurate, accurate, and very accurate. The sample includes only posts without user comments (i.e., the control condition). The figure pools posts from the UK, Italy, and Germany, displaying short titles. The full text of all posts with translations is available in the online appendix.

melts glaciers," "Lauterbach almost abducted," "Monkeypox emergency US," "Putin recruits children").

A challenge for any work focusing on social media content is choosing what content to include in experimental studies. We would like to reiterate that we do not claim that the set of headlines we have selected for inclusion in our study is a random sample of all content. Thus, we discourage any interpretation that focuses on how much people generally believe or do not believe social media headlines *in general*. However, we do believe that our broader-than-average pool of headlines allows us to make more generalizable claims about what factors are associated with perceived accuracy.

2.3 The Correlates of Believing Online Content

What factors are associated with believing – or disbelieving – the content we see online? As a general rule, people are biased toward accepting incoming information (Brashier & Marsh, 2020). There are perhaps many competing and complementary explanations for this predilection to *generally* accept claims as true – most claims we encounter are true, telling the truth is a societal norm,

Figure 2 Example of a social media post used in Italy (false news). False news post identified as accurate by the smallest share of respondents. Translation: "Italy is already at war; the army heads toward Russia's new campaign."

Figure 3 Example of a social media post used in the UK (false news). COP26 jets emit tons of CO2. False news that is identified as accurate by highest share of respondents.

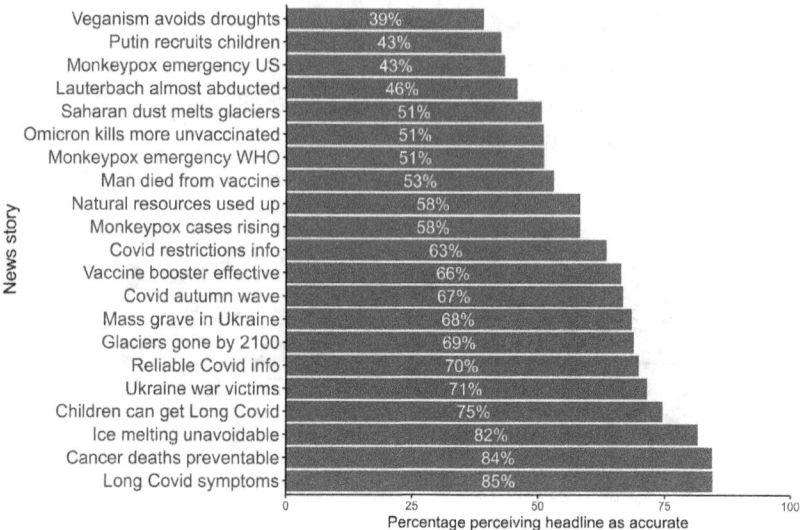

Figure 4 Percentage of true news headlines perceived as accurate or very accurate (combined share). Respondents rated all posts on a four-point scale: not at all accurate, not accurate, accurate, and very accurate. The sample includes only posts without user comments (i.e., the control condition). The figure pools posts from the UK, Italy, and Germany, displaying short titles. The full text of all posts with translations is available in the online appendix.

rejecting and/or counterarguing the content we see online takes cognitive effort, and so on (Schwarz et al., 2016; Abeler et al., 2019). In this section, we examine the factors associated with believing online content, and the extent to which these markers are similar for true and false content.

2.3.1 Believing False Online Content

The ideological alignment of a post with a respondent's beliefs – the first factor we consider here – is significantly associated with the acceptance of false news and other forms of false content (Bryanov & Vziatysheva, 2021). Individuals are more likely to believe information that is in line with existing beliefs (see Garrett, 2011; Moravec et al., 2018; Kim & Dennis, 2019; Kim et al., 2019; Bago & Pennycook, 2020). Other work shows that individuals continue to believe false content even after it is flagged as such if it aligns with their preexisting beliefs (Moravec et al., 2018). Ideological orientations structure citizens' views in politics and also matter when it comes to misinformation (Garrett, 2011; Buchanan, 2020). There is some evidence that conservatives or

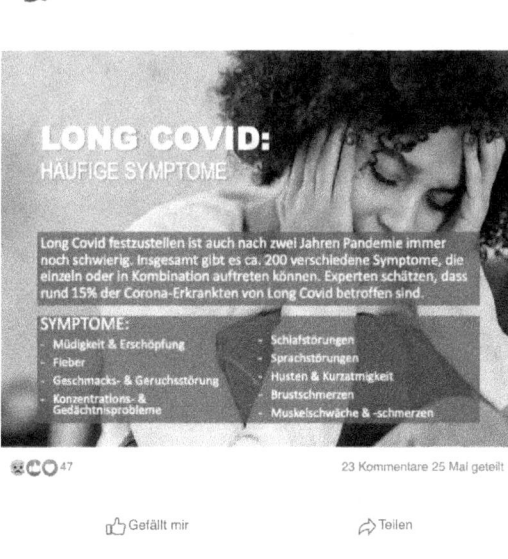

Figure 5 Example of a social media post used in Germany (true news). Long Covid symptoms. True news considered accurate by highest share of respondents. Translation: "Long Covid: common symptoms; after two years of the pandemic, it is still difficult to detect long Covid. (...)"

right-leaning individuals tend to believe and engage more with misinformation than liberals (Guess et al., 2019; Buchanan, 2020; Osmundsen et al., 2021; Pretus et al., 2023). While accuracy prompts appear to be a promising way to affect how people evaluate false content (Pennycook & Rand, 2021), there is also some evidence that individuals with far-right positions may not respond to this type of intervention (Pretus et al., 2023).

Given the rise of populist politicians and parties, it is useful to go beyond a one-dimensional conception of ideology and account for an additional anti-expert dimension (Uscinski et al., 2021). This dimension is particularly important given Europe's multiparty systems and multidimensional space of party competition. There is some evidence that anti-expert sentiments are frequently associated with misperceptions (Chinn & Hasell, 2023; Spälti et al., 2023).

Other individual-level variation also affects how people evaluate false claims. For instance, cognitive reflection capabilities are also considered to potentially influence people's evaluation of misinformation. Having higher cognitive reflection skills means that a person is more likely to deliberately reflect on an issue. To

Figure 6 Example of a social media post used in Germany (true news). True news considered accurate by a comparatively small share of respondents. Headline translation: "Putin recruits and raises his future soldiers in Ukrainian Mariupol. (...)"

measure this trait, respondents of a survey answer questions that seem to have an obvious, but incorrect, answer. To give the right response, it is necessary to take a moment and think harder about the problem (Pennycook & Rand, 2019b, 2020). Scoring high on cognitive reflection tests is related to a better ability to recognize misinformation in survey and experimental settings (Pennycook & Rand, 2019a, 2019b; Ali & Qazi, 2022). Importantly, people with high-cognitive reflection follow and post more high-quality news (Mosleh et al., 2021) and appear to consume less untrustworthy online content (Guess et al., 2020). On the other hand, individuals with low-cognitive reflection capacities are more prone to nudging (Schulz et al., 2018).

While many studies find that more educated individuals are less susceptible to misinformation, results on this question do exhibit some inconsistency (Nan et al., 2022). When it comes to sharing or reposting misinformation, Buchanan (2020) explains that less educated survey respondents are more likely to do so, according to self-reports. More educated individuals tend to engage more in correcting other users, according to findings by Bode and Vraga (2021a, 2021b).

The role of age for susceptibility to misinformation is contested. For instance, Pehlivanoglu and colleagues (2022) do find age to play a role, albeit the oldest individuals seem to have difficulties detecting false news. At times, young participants report sharing more misinformation than older ones (Buchanan, 2020). In other surveys, however, a strong age effect has been observed, for example, during the 2016 presidential election in the United States (Guess et al., 2019; Osmundsen et al., 2021). Lyons et al. (2024) also note a discrepancy between surveys and (behavioral) tracing data.

Finally, we turn to susceptibility to social influence (SSI) as a trait whose link to believing false news has received less attention. SSI measures how easily other people's actions can prompt an individual to adapt their behavior and attitudes (Stöckli & Hofer, 2020). This approach builds on a rich literature about the importance of social groups for individual behavior (Asch 1956; Cialdini & Goldstein, 2004) and has recently focused on its importance in online environments. For instance, SSI predicts several aspects of social media behavior, such as liking or buying products that other users suggested (Stöckli & Hofer, 2020). Several studies find critical comments to impact individuals' perception of the veracity of news content, which the authors attribute to social influence (Winter et al., 2015; Colliander, 2019). Castellini et al. (2021) link SSI to believing misinformation about food. Other research comes to different conclusions. For instance, Mena et al. (2020) show that people are more likely to believe misinformation after celebrity endorsement on Instagram than if a post receives a high number of likes.

2.3.2 Believing True Online Content

As noted above, individuals are predisposed to believe new information they encounter because, statistically, most of it will be true (Brashier & Marsh, 2020). Nonetheless, recent studies observe increasing skepticism toward the media (Michael & Breaux, 2021; Hameleers et al., 2022). Digital literacy interventions have been shown to generate skepticism of the accuracy of both mainstream news and false content while also increasing discernment between the two (e.g., Guess et al. 2020).

Importantly, the factors that determine believing misinformation may differ from those that affect belief in accurate information. Individuals tend to only struggle with one of the two (Bronstein et al., 2019; Pennycook & Rand, 2020; Sindermann et al., 2021). In contrast to digital literacy interventions that may generally increase skepticism for all forms of content, a critical thinking intervention (Lutzke et al., 2019) appears to make people less susceptible to false news, without similarly affecting perceptions of accurate news.

Indeed, there is good evidence that there might be different antecedents to how people perceive and evaluate accurate and inaccurate information. Several traits are found to correlate with disbelieving true news, such as (low) interpersonal trust and having a more right-wing ideology (Michael & Breaux, 2021). Michael and Breaux (2021) observe a similar effect using ideology in place of values, demonstrating that Americans on the political left believe more true news, while right-identifying study participants labelled more news as false and/or propaganda.

Currently, a significant part of the literature considers discernment rather than the relationship between believing false news and disbelieving factually correct information (see Pennycook & Rand, 2019a, 2019b; Roozenbeek et al., 2022; Epstein et al., 2023). Discernment denotes how capable a person is of distinguishing between true and false news. However, it does not offer any insights on who (dis-)believes which kind of information. For example, the partisan bias mentioned does not have an impact on truth discernment overall, because it has opposite effects based on whether information is congruent or incongruent with an individual's beliefs (Gawronski, 2021).

2.4 The Correlates of Belief in False and True News in Our Data

We use key variables mentioned in the literature to examine susceptibility to the false news stories in our sample, and we use the same predictors to analyze disbelief in true news (e.g., Pennycook & Rand, 2019b; Bryanov & Vziatysheva, 2021; Lyons et al., 2021). We find patterns that are consistent with the literature and we also unearth novel findings (Figure 7). Respondents are more likely to consider false news as accurate when the information is in line with their attitude toward that issue (e.g., individuals who do not find vaccines helpful are more likely to consider misinformation about vaccines to be true; for more information on our measure for ideological alignment, see Section 3 and the online appendix for our coding). The strongest predictor in the model is a far-right ideological position; far-right positions are associated with a greater likelihood to find false news accurate. Anti-expert positions are also linked to a greater likelihood of believing false news. In our data, older respondents are better equipped to identify false news. Here, it is important to note the above mentioned discrepancy with digital trace data: While older individuals are often better at identifying false news in surveys, they seem to share false news more often according to behavioral data (Lyons et al., 2024). Cognitive reflection capabilities help people to identify false news as well. We do not find that education levels and gender are associated with variation in accuracy perceptions.

What about disbelieving true news? Are the predictors that explain false news susceptibility also linked to disbelief in true news? Here, we find a more mixed picture. Ideological alignment of information plays a similar role on both sides. For instance, when a story is ideologically aligned – i.e. in line with preexisting beliefs – individuals are more able to conceive it to be true, irrespective of

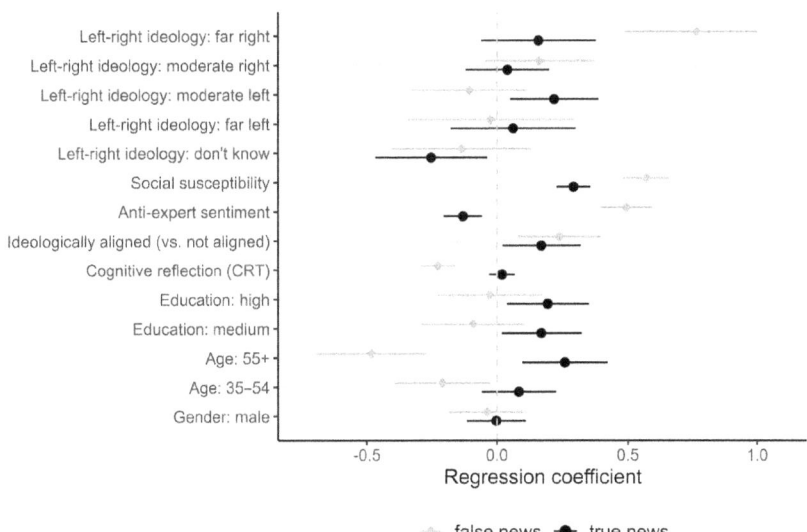

Figure 7 The correlates of false and true news susceptibility. Authors' data. Multilevel model with post ratings nested within individuals. N (false news posts) = 6,663, N (true news posts) = 7,154. Outcome is perceived accuracy of a social media post (range = not at all accurate, not accurate, accurate, very accurate). Lines show 95 percent confidence intervals.

veracity: That is, the effect holds for false and true information. Individuals who score high on SSI are also more likely to find true as well as false news accurate. This means that they are more likely to identify false news incorrectly, because it is assumed to be accurate.

Individuals who score high on anti-expert sentiments are more likely to believe that false news is accurate but less likely to find true news accuracy. Hence, they are more likely to incorrectly identify information on both counts. While we find that people are less likely to believe false news, they are more likely to find true news accurate. Cognitive reflection skills make it less likely for people to identify false news as true but not more likely to identify true news as accurate. People with higher levels of education are more likely to consider accurate information as true. When it comes to ideology (beyond anti-expert sentiments), we find that individuals without party attachment are significantly less likely to identify true news as accurate. Individuals with moderate left leaning views are more likely to rate true news as accurate.

2.5 Conclusion

Based on the false and true news that we use as material in our experiments, we can show much variation in belief in false news and disbelief in true news. If individuals are asked to rate the accuracy of a set of true news and false news stories, we find that some false stories are considered accurate by a much larger share of people than others. The difference that we document is large; all false news stories are considered accurate by at least one fifth of respondents, while some are considered accurate by a much larger share. In a similar vein, a lot of true news stories are considered accurate and there is also much variation. We also find important regularities among the characteristics that are associated with the extent to which people find information accurate, irrespective of whether it is true or false. For instance, individuals are more likely to find ideologically aligned news stories more accurate, irrespective of veracity. In contrast, anti-expert sentiments increase the likelihood of an individual finding false news accurate and true news inaccurate.

3 The Core Experimental Setup

Our main research question is whether corrective user comments help people to recognize inaccurate content. We also want to understand how miscorrections affect users in the context of true news. We conducted a survey experiment in which respondents are randomly assigned to social media posts with and without comments. Respondents took part in a survey that included a set of pretreatment questions and exposed them to a set of nine social media posts (Figure 8). Some of these posts were false news posts and others were true news posts. After seeing each social media post, respondents were asked to rate how accurate they found each post. We also asked whether they would "like" or share them on social media. At the end of the survey, respondents were debriefed. The debriefing highlighted which social media posts included false information and provided links to fact checks. The survey questionnaires along with translations are shown in the online appendix. We build on the experimental setup first presented in Stoeckel et al. (2024), but significantly extend the analysis – most importantly, by additionally accounting for the ideological alignment between respondents and the information they assess.

The experimental design allows us to test the causal role of comments. Respondents either rated the control condition version of a social media post or one of the treatment conditions that included corrective comments (in the case of false news) or miscorrections (in the case of true news). If social corrections are effective, we would expect accuracy ratings to be lower when respondents are exposed to social media posts that include corrective comments (i.e., when they are in a treatment condition) rather than when they do not see corrections (i.e., when they are in the control condition). If miscorrections work in a similar way, we would expect users to consider true social

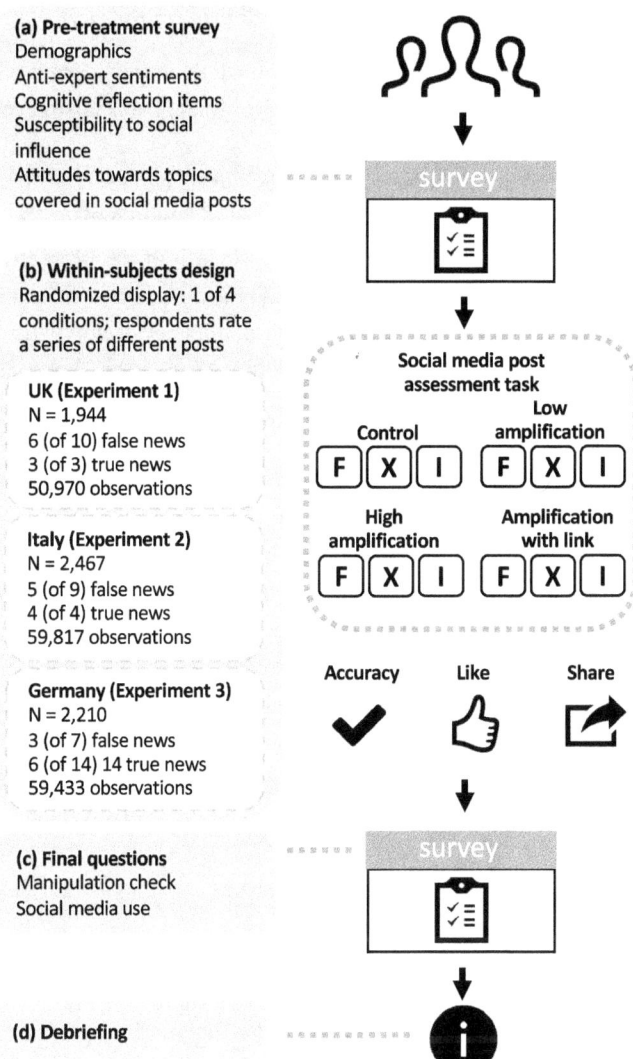

Figure 8 Research design used for fieldwork in the UK, Italy, and Germany. The fieldwork included the following parts in each country: (a) participants responded to a set of pretreatment questions; (b) they assessed randomly assigned social media content from four conditions (false news: control, a correction with low amplification, a correction with high amplification, or a correction with link; true news: control, miscorrection with low amplification, miscorrection with high amplification, or a miscorrection with link). Respondents assessed the accuracy of each post, the probability of "liking" it, and the probability of sharing it. Next, (c) participants answered a set of final questions and were (d) debriefed (the debriefing included information indicating posts that were debunked). F: Facebook, X: previously Twitter, I: Instagram. See the online appendix for details on each condition in the UK, Germany, and Italy.

media posts less accurate when accompanied with comments from other users which say that the information shown in the original post is false (even though it is in fact true).

Our design choices are influenced by previous research, so before addressing our design we quickly review the literature. Previous studies come to different conclusions about the role of the strength of the corrective signal, for example, whether a single comment already affects user comments or whether there need to be many corrective comments or sophisticated ones which also substantiate the correction with a link. This is an important question also for the development of best practice strategies for those who want to write effective corrections. For instance, Vraga and Bode (2017) find that a single user correction is not effective. Two user comments have been found to be effective, but Vraga and Bode (2018, p. 1346) stress the importance of a link that bolsters a comment: "it seems that when everyday users are correcting one another, the provision of a source confirming the correction being offered is required." More recent research from India finds that simple corrections can be effective and the presence of a fact-checking link is neither needed in order for a correction to be effective nor does it add power to the effect of a correction (Badrinathan & Chauchard, 2023). This is in line with other recent research from the US, which finds that the presence of a correction is more important than the tone or style of it (Tully, Bode & Vraga, 2020).

In our experiments, we examine a variety of versions of corrections and miscorrections (see the online appendix for a detailed overview). In all countries, we use treatments which increase the "signal strength" of a correction from a weaker signal to what might be a stronger signal. We do this in order to test if variation in the signal strength or the complexity of the corrective comments makes comments more effective. We therefore use different versions of our treatments: a low amplification condition where the correction by users is not amplified, a high amplification where the corrective signal is amplified in different ways, and a condition that includes a link to a fact-checking website. One way the corrective signal is amplified is by increasing the number of likes on corrective comments. We test this in the fieldwork in the UK. In the fieldwork in Italy and Germany, we test whether increasing the signal strength via the number of corrective comments from few (low amplification) to many (high amplification) leads to greater treatment effects. Additionally, we test if corrections and miscorrections are more effective when they include links to a fact-checking website (amplification with link). In Germany, we also test whether attributing true news to a media outlet via a source cue reduces the impact of miscorrections. To foreshadow the results: these differences are largely irrelevant, which is in line with what Badrinathan and Chauchard (2023) found. However, the results still help us to better understand the way social media users are likely to process the content of comments.

3.1 Material

The content of our material was taken from real-world social media posts. Thus, we did not create false news for the purposes of our experiments. We used a social media simulator (https://zeoob.com/) to generate the treatment material based on existing posts and to design the various treatment versions. Every post was generated in four versions (control and three treatment conditions). To maximize external validity, our treatment material shows comments written and posted by social media users, though these comments are not necessarily from the posts that we display. We did not use the original names of people who posted the stories we use, but generated names with another simulator (https://britishsurnames.co.uk/random). For profile pictures, we rely on material from the Flickr-Faces-HQ Dataset (FFHQ) (Karras et al., 2019). We created a post with the original claim and used those as post for all treatment conditions. Features of a post (online user status, activiation of fields, location tags, etc.) were kept constant across posts and conditions.

In all countries, we used a treatment condition where corrective and miscorrective comments respectively include a link. In the case of false news, these are links to websites that officially debunk content. (e.g., from https://fullfact.org/). In the case of true news, miscorrections include a link to a website that seemingly bolsters the (false) claim of the miscorrection.

3.1.1 Corrections from Unknown Users?

Our analysis focuses on social media content and on the role of content from people who are strangers to the viewer, rather than friends or family. While this is relevant to consider, we believe that this would create more conservative effects – that is, we are more likely to underestimate the effect of corrections, rather than overestimate them, because signals from unknown individuals are likely to be less effective than signals from known others. Most importantly, focusing on correction from unknown sources is important in its own right, since today's social media landscape is not solely made up of interactions with close social contacts, but there is a lot of exposure to content by strangers (Anspach, 2017; Anspach & Carlson, 2020).

Even if other users are not known to an individual, their contributions – content or comments – might not necessarily be perceived as coming from a complete stranger. Despite not knowing them, there may be some weak links by being part of a "social media crowd" (Margolin & Liao, 2018). Social media publics can, for instance, form around social issues or attitudes (Jackson & Foucault Welles, 2015; Carter & Alford, 2023). Individuals with similar attitudes to what is expressed in critical comments may identify themselves with an unknown commenter, which could establish a weak link. Such weak links have been shown to be important ties (Granovetter, 1973; Kaplan, 2021). This is supported by a study on US presidential approval ratings by Anspach and Carlson (2020, p. 714), who find that people are more likely "to cite information provided by social media posters as accurate than the information contained in article previews."

An individual may care about strangers' comments. Friends are often intuitively regarded as epistemic peers, meaning that we see them as equally able to distinguish between correct and false information. This may influence our perception of how informed our friends are on an issue (Elga, 2007; Margolin, Hannak & Weber, 2018). Lupia and McCubbins (1998) consider this perceived level of expertise more important than someone's actual knowledge in persuasion. If we do not know a lot about a certain topic, we may expect the same from close social contacts. In such cases, we are still more likely to follow our own opinion when we disagree with friends. A friend's comment may even be less effective if we do not have reason to believe that they would be more informed than us. However, when encountering comments from strangers online, individuals may hesitate to dismiss them outright – not necessarily because they see these strangers as more knowledgeable, but because they have little information about their level of expertise. Online, it is difficult for people to identify the level of expertise of unknown others. If multiple people online repeat the same information, this might also create an impression of broader consensus or credibility. As a result, individuals may not fully want to disregard a stranger's opinions (Anspach & Carlson, 2020). Thus, one of the reasons why strangers' comments might matter could be perceived levels of expertise, or because individuals find the views of others an important peer signal that serves as a heuristic (a discussion we return to at the beginning of Section 4).

There may also be a difference in societal pressure. As Margolin, Hannak, and Weber (2018) point out, this is emphasized when people are corrected directly by a friend because they would not want their reputation to be damaged. When viewing strangers' corrections of other people's posts, this effect may not be present to the same extent. However, pressure to fit into society in general is a major motivation in people's lives (Krech, Crutchfield

& Ballachey, 1962). If the same corrective message is repeatedly observed on different platforms, conformity pressure could cause people to start believing it (Zhao, 2019). Similarly, false news with a satirical origin is shared less once people realize where it came from, likely to save their reputation (Shin et al., 2017). Hence, social pressure among friends may be strong, but pressure to conform more broadly can also be observed among strangers. The evidence for the role that social norms play for the dissemination of false news on social media is, however, mixed (Gimpel et al., 2021; Epstein et al., 2021; Prike et al. 2024).

Since contact with strangers on social media is common, weak links may be perceived between unknown commenters and readers if they are part of the same social media crowd, strengthening the comment's influence (Margolin & Liao, 2018). Moreover, close social contacts may be considered epistemic peers, while strangers could be perceived as knowledgeable (Anspach & Carlson, 2020).

3.2 Dependent Variables

3.2.1 Accuracy Perceptions of News Headlines

The main outcome we are interested in is perceived accuracy of content that people find on social media. We analyze if people are able to spot the low accuracy of false content and our experiments are about whether social corrections help them in that regard. We are also interested in perceived accuracy of true content and how miscorrections affect these perceptions, which is covered by our experiments as well. Our measure is a four point scale with the following response categories: not at all accurate, not accurate, accurate, and very accurate. It is important to acknowledge that we ask respondents to rate the accuracy of false and true news headlines (rather than, for instance, a full article), in line with a large body of research on social media news perceptions (see Neubaum & Krämer, 2017; Vraga & Bode, 2017; Colliander, 2019; Lyons et al., 2021; Epstein et al., 2023). This approach also maximizes both internal and external validity. For instance, a lot of links are shared just based on headlines (Gabielkov et al., 2016). Moreover, this approach gets more directly at the core of the problem, because users who hesitate to assess the validity of content just based on a headline are less likely to drive the dissemination of false information (Spezzano et al., 2021).

3.2.2 Not Just Accuracy: The Role of Liking and Sharing

While our primary focus is on the relationship between social corrections and accuracy perceptions, we also focus on two additional outcomes: the intention of users to like and share content on social media. The ability of users to easily share posts is in fact one of the reasons why false information can spread particularly quickly on social media (Lazer et al., 2018; Vosoughi, Roy & Aral, 2018; Tully, Bode & Vraga, 2020). Other ways of engagement with social media content, such as when users "like" it by clicking the respective button, can lead to (mis)information being more salient as well (Lazer et al., 2018; Buchanan, 2020).

One should note, however, that there are a variety of reasons why users might like or share content – and engaging with posts does not necessarily imply approval or considering information to be accurate. Indeed, one of the main reasons why misinformation is so prevalent is that people share it without reflecting on its accuracy (Pennycook & Rand, 2021; Pennycook et al., 2021b). Because it seems like the sharer approves of the content, other users may also be more inclined to pay heed to the false news (Lazer et al., 2018). Another common reason for sharing misinformation is its entertainment potential and novelty. As long as misinformation is more noteworthy, it tends to disseminate further (Chen et al., 2015; Vosoughi, Roy & Aral, 2018; King et al., 2021).

While existing work focuses on the effect of comments on accuracy perceptions (see Vraga & Bode, 2017; Zhang et al., 2022), there is some evidence that comments also affect liking and sharing. Boot, Dijkstra, and Zwaan (2021) find that Dutch students were less likely to share news content if critical comments had been posted, even if they were complemented by the same number or positive comments or were clearly subjective. Similarly, Colliander (2019) observed a decrease in sharing intention when corrective comments were present. In contrast, Friggeri et al. (2014) traced rumors on Facebook to observe how they develop and how debunking impacts them. Users were found to be less likely to reshare misinformation once comments contain links to fact-checking websites.

Other studies found that tweets debunking misinformation were reposted more frequently than the original post in some cases (Takayasu et al., 2015; Chua et al., 2017). However, this does not appear to always be the case, as Wang and Zhuang (2018) found that over 78 percent of people did not clarify or delete the misinformation they posted after being debunked. The varying results may be due to the different sources of the corrective comments, as such social aspects play an important role in debunking (Margolin, Hannak & Weber, 2018). Most notably, it was found in the past that corrections by an official source are more effective than ones by the public (Vraga & Bode, 2017; Hunt, Wang & Zhuang, 2020; Wang, 2021).

Concerning the effect of likes, Boot, Dijkstra, and, Zwaan (2021, p. 8) found that "the presence of Likes had no effect on the readers' content evaluation."

This is supported by other studies that did not find a statistically significant effect when the number of likes for news posts (Winter, Brückner & Krämer, 2015; Neubaum & Krämer, 2017) or for the critical comments (Masullo & Kim, 2021) was varied. This stands in conflict with other studies who state that critical comments with more likes (Naab et al., 2020) or news content with more likes (Luo, Hancock & Markowitz, 2022) influenced people's perceptions of the news articles. Hence, while the literature recognizes the potential of likes as social cues (Naab et al., 2020; Wang, 2021; Luo, Hancock & Markowitz, 2022), they were not found to have a considerable impact in most studies (Waddell, 2020).

Overall, critical comments appear to have stronger effects than likes. Likes are presented in numerical form, so some of the literature cites the abstractness of numbers as a possible reason for this (Winter, Brückner & Krämer, 2015; Neubaum & Krämer, 2017). The contextuality of likes may also have contributed to their modest influence, since some accounts always get more than others. Alternative possibilities are that likes are a positive cue while people place more emphasis on negative ones (Winter, Brückner & Krämer, 2015). This is further supported by Boot, Dijkstra, and Zwaan (2021) who find a similar phenomenon in relation to comments (only negative ones influence people's perceptions of news content).

Epstein et al. (2023) report that participants had greater difficulty distinguishing between true and false information when they were asked both to assess accuracy and to indicate their likelihood of sharing a post. This raises concerns about our decision to ask respondents about both accuracy and engagement (liking or sharing), as doing so may influence their judgment. However, while Epstein and colleagues show that responses can vary depending on whether one or both questions are posed, they do not establish which method best reflects real-world behavior – that is, which is more externally valid. In fact, there is a case to be made for including both measures. Epstein et al. (2023, p. 5) write that the "spillover effect [asking both outcomes] suggests that the social media context – and the mindset that it produces – actively interferes with accuracy discernment." This is highly relevant to our study: (a) sharing is central to how social media functions, and (b) our experimental intervention targets accuracy perceptions. Therefore, if social motivations are activated and we still observe positive effects of social corrections, it lends additional strength to our findings.[1]

---

[1] Based on our data, we are not in a position to definitively address the concerns raised by Epstein and colleagues (2023) regarding whether the inclusion of multiple outcome measures – such as accuracy and sharing intentions – might alter the observed effects of user corrections. It remains unclear whether limiting the design to a single outcome would substantially affect the size, direction, or statistical significance of our findings. While we do not expect major changes, we acknowledge that others might view this differently, and we recognize that this remains an open question for future research to explore.

3.3 Moderators: Anti-expert Sentiments, Cognitive Reflection, and Susceptibility to Social Influence

In addition to testing the main effects, we also examine whether the treatment effects vary depending on respondents' cognitive reflection capabilities, their susceptibility to social influence, and anti-expert sentiments. These variables correlate with the ability of people to identify false information (Section 2), but these variables might also condition the effect of our treatments. For instance, individuals with stronger cognitive reflection skills might be more likely to take comments into account when reading a post and they might not be taken into account at all by those with low cognitive reflection skills. If that is the case, they would only be effective among those with moderate or strong cognitive reflection skills. We use a common measure for cognitive reflection skills that combines four items (Pennycook & Rand, 2019b). Each of these items has an answer that might intuitively be right but is in fact wrong, and careful reflection helps to answer correctly. For instance, one of the questions is the following: "If you're running a race and you pass the person in second place, what place are you in?" The answer options are first, second, third, or fourth (with "second" being the correct answer).

In a similar vein, we test if susceptibility to social influence and anti-expert sentiments moderate the role of the treatments. Individuals who are more susceptible to social influence might be more affected by other users' reactions to content, and therefore react more strongly to signals from others. This variable also helps us to better understand the mechanism through which corrections might work: If corrections work because people align their views to accuracy perceptions of others, one could expect those who place greater care more about the views of others generally to exhibit greater treatment effects. We measure susceptibility to social influence using a seven-item scale (Stöckli et al., 2020), which includes items such as: "I based my decisions on information I gain from online social network posts and interactions" (with a five point response scale that ranges from strong agreement to strong disagreement). Finally, we test if the effect of the treatment differs depending on the strength of respondents' anti-expert sentiments. People who see experts negatively might be less receptive to other people's knowledge and their messages about content accuracy. We use a common measure from the literature that combines three items; for example, "I am more confident in my opinion than other people's facts" (Han et al., 2022; Spälti et al., 2023). We also phrased our expectation for an interaction as a hypothesis for the fieldwork in the UK, and as a research question in the subsequent fieldwork in Italy and Germany.

3.4 Fieldwork

3.4.1 UK

Respondents were recruited via Dynata with country specific quotas on gender, age, education, and region in the UK, Italy, and Germany. Thus, the samples reflect the respective populations with regard to these characteristics. Our British fieldwork took place in July 2022 (N = 1,944, 50.9% f, 48.7% m, 0.4% non-binary, third gender, and other). In the UK, the first treatment condition includes a corrective comment with just a few likes (low amplification). In the second condition, we increase the signal of the correction by showing a higher number of likes (high amplification condition: the corrective comment shows up to 190 likes). A manipulation check showed that respondents perceived a difference between comments with few and many likes. That is, we showed a comment ("There is something deeply deeply fishy about this") with only ten "likes" (low amplification) and the same comment with 184 "likes" (high amplification) and asked respondents to indicate how strongly they perceive the support from other users (1 = very weak; 5 = very strong). The high amplification condition is perceived as receiving significantly more support from other users than the low amplification condition, which supports our operationalization (Ms (SDs) = 3.02 (1.15) vs. 2.77 (1.13); t = 6.17, p < 0.001). This difference did not translate into an effect on accuracy perception or one of the other outcomes, which is why we tested the role of another amplification of corrections in Italy and Germany. The third treatment condition increases the corrective signal further: The corrective comment includes up to 190 likes, such as in the high amplification condition, and additionally shows a fact-checking link, following the argument by Bode and Vraga (2017) that a source might be crucial for corrective comments to be effective.

Our "miscorrection" experimental stimuli mirror this structure. That is, the low amplification condition includes a miscorrection with few likes and the high amplification condition includes a miscorrection with many likes (same range as in the case of false news). The condition with a fact-checking link leads to a website that seemingly bolsters the miscorrection.

3.4.2 Italy

We conducted our fieldwork in Italy in August 2022 (N = 2,467, 49.1% f, 50.5% m, 0.3% non-binary, third gender, and other). Just as in the UK, a simulation-based power analysis showed that we needed a sample of N = 1,800 (see our preregistration for details).

While the main building blocks of our experimental setup is similar across countries, we also implemented slight changes. As in the UK, respondents in the control condition do not see any corrective comments. The treatment conditions increase the signal strength of the correction or miscorrection respectively in all three countries. However, rather than increasing the number of likes as in the UK, in Italy (and in Germany) we showed more corrective comments in the high amplification condition (see the online appendix for the full specification of each condition). More corrective comments take up more space visually, which could make the amplification more salient than just showing many likes.

Specifically, the first treatment condition includes a user comment that corrects inaccurate information present in a post. In order to increase external validity, we show another comment which does not refute the original (inaccurate) message of the post. Thus, the correction in this condition is a relatively weak signal, as comments are mixed when it comes to the original post. The second treatment condition includes more corrective comments, along with a user comment that does not correct the post. We also test a third condition, which resembles the low amplification condition, but additionally includes a link to a fact-checking website.

The miscorrections in the case of true news follow a similar pattern. We show a low amplification condition with just one miscorrection and a high amplification condition with two miscorrective comments. A third condition additionally includes a link to a website that seems to bolster the miscorrection.

3.4.3 Germany

The fieldwork in Germany took place in January and February 2023 ($N = 2,210$, 50.3% f, 49.4% m, 0.3% non-binary, third gender, and other). The fieldwork resembles the Italian fieldwork, especially with regard to false news (we use a low amplification condition, a high amplification condition, and a condition with link to a fact-check website). However, there is also an important innovation in the context of true news that we did not test in the UK or Italy: We additionally took into account the role of sources. In the UK and Italy, true news posts did not include source cues which would tell respondents where information in a post is from. Yet, showing true news without a source cue might create an artificial situation rather than one social media users find often in reality. In Germany, we test whether miscorrections affect users even when a source cue is displayed in one of the conditions. Thus, we can test if miscorrections affect users despite them seeing the media outlet from which a piece of information originates. In Germany, our design uses a control condition as in Italy and the UK, and three treatment conditions: We show a high amplification condition that includes a source cue for the origin of the original piece of (true) news (includes several miscorrection comments), a high amplification condition without source cue (includes several miscorrection comments), and a high amplification condition with link to a fact-checking website.

3.5 Modeling

We preregistered all fieldwork on OSF (UK: https://osf.io/fpm2e/?view_only=1f2999c931c84404bddd618ce33208bd; Italy: https://osf.io/upzm8/?view_only=55393ea5c1634c2ea87c793f0cfc07d3; Germany: https://osf.io/rfq6h/?view_only=26e88087c3c442ff810b6ce452736e75). We preregistered the fieldwork separately for each country, with the first fieldwork in the UK informing our preregistrations for fieldwork in Italy and Germany. The preregistrations specify hypotheses for the main effects as well as for interactions. As shown in our previous work (Stoeckel et al., 2024), the results hold when not controlling for ideological alignment. In order to probe the results further, we present analyses in Section 4 that additionally control for ideological alignment of the content that respondents assessed (which is a substantively important deviation from the preregistrations).

Each respondent rated a set of nine social media posts, which allows us to leverage a within subjects design. We employed a randomization at the level of posts, that is, respondents could see each post either in the control or in one of the three treatment conditions. In order to model this data structure, we use linear mixed-effects models as specified in the preregistrations. Mixed-effects models account for a data structure in which observations (assessments of posts) are nested within individuals (Steenbergen & Jones, 2002). We run separate analyses for each country.

For the main effect of social corrections on the three response variables of interest – perceived accuracy, probability to "like", and probability to share false news – we entered the social correction treatment (4-level factor) as main predictor into a model. We also added demographics as covariates (age, gender, education).

Our models also control for ideological alignment of news stories (albeit the results hold if ideological alignment is excluded; Stoeckel et al., 2024). Controlling for ideological alignment allows us to account for the fact that individuals are more likely to find information accurate if it aligns with their beliefs or opinions. In research in the US context, a common procedure to control for ideological alignment is to account for the party affiliation of respondents (Lyons et al., 2021). In our case, we asked respondents pretreatment questions about the topics that come up in the treatment material. For instance, we would ask respondents their view on COVID-19 vaccines. Misinformation that portrays COVID-19 vaccines as harmful would be ideologically aligned for individuals who see vaccines negatively. By controlling for ideological alignment, we can test the robustness of social corrections even when they are not ideologically aligned. The ideological alignment measures for each social media post can be found in the online appendix.

The model includes random intercepts for both respondents and social media posts to account for the nested structure of the data. We apply the same modeling approach when analyzing the effects of miscorrections on perceptions of true news.

Response ~ social correction treatment + gender + age + education + ideological alignment + (1|respondent id) + (1|social media post)

We also examine whether treatment effects vary across individual characteristics – specifically anti-expert sentiments, cognitive reflection (CRT), and susceptibility to social influence (SSI). To do so, we estimate interaction models that include each individual difference measure and its interaction with the social correction treatment:

response ~ social correction treatment * individual difference measure + gender + age+ education + (1|respondent id) + (1|social media post)

Identifying interaction effects typically requires larger sample sizes than detecting main effects. Therefore, our power calculations focused on ensuring sufficient statistical power to detect a small interaction between social corrections and individual-level moderators, such as susceptibility to social influence or anti-expert attitudes. The linear mixed-effects model treats perceived accuracy as a repeated measure and includes a random intercept for each social media post. Based on pilot data, and assuming an effect size of –0.07 for the difference in slope between the control condition and the high amplification + link condition, we determined that a minimum sample size of 1,800 respondents would be necessary to achieve 80 percent statistical power (see preregistration for further details).

4 Social Corrections, Miscorrections, and Accuracy Perceptions

The main question that we seek to answer is whether user-written comments that correct false social media posts help people to identify inaccurate social media content. In a similar vein, we are interested in whether miscorrections – comments that raise doubts about true information – affect accuracy perception of social media content as well. Our research design also includes several treatment conditions, which help us to understand the relevance of the strength of corrections and format. We use these results and analyses of a series of heterogeneous treatment effects to improve our understanding of the mechanism that explains how individuals form accuracy perceptions and the role that user comments play in this context. We begin by outlining the mechanisms that have been discussed in the literature.

4.1 A Debate on the Mechanism

Several mechanisms are discussed in the literature that could explain why corrective comments from other users might affect accuracy perceptions of content that users see on social media. There are key differences across potential mechanisms regarding the extent to which users process information. According to one set of studies, users process both the content of a post as well as contextual information such as comments, and features of these comments, such as their source or credibility (e.g., Vraga & Bode, 2017; Colliander, 2019; Badrinathan & Chauchard, 2023). Thus, there is a possibility that comments are processed in a central or systematic manner. We discuss the related approaches in Sections 4.1.1 and 4.1.2. An alternative assumption is that users do not in fact spend a lot of cognitive resources on both the content and comments, which has consequences for the way corrections (and miscorrections) affect users (e.g., Haugtvedt and Wegener; 1994; Anspach & Carlson, 2020). We briefly outline the related mechanisms in Sections 4.1.3 and 4.1.4. As with any mental process, it is difficult to directly test the mechanism that drives the effect of social corrections. That said, we can use our data to shed light on this issue. The results from subgroup analyses do not support the notion of users processing social media content and related comments in a central way; instead, it seems more likely that processing is superficial and recency effects dominate.

4.1.1 Source Credibility

We begin with approaches that assume that user comments are processed cognitively to at least some degree, allowing certain content features – e.g., credibility – to matter. We then move on to approaches that assume that comments are processed superficially. Vraga and Bode (2017) highlight that corrective comments might derive their effectiveness from the perceived credibility of a corrective message, rather than just the presence of a corrective comment itself. Hence, corrective comments need to be perceived as credible in order to influence users. In a situation where users look at corrective comments from other people they do not know, credibility can be provided by corrective comments that include a source to back up the claim in a correction (e.g., a link to a fact-checking website). Indeed, Vraga and Bode (2017) find that only corrections with a source are effective in their study, which examines the case of misinformation on the Zika virus in the US. A meta-study also concludes that source credibility matters: Walter et al. (2021) note that social corrections originating from an expert are more effective than those from an anonymous user. Further research compares the effectiveness of corrections from users with warnings from algorithms. Bode and Vraga (2018) find social corrections equally effective as warnings, while Zeng et al. (2024) report some evidence that users may be more effective.

4.1.2 Peer Group Signals

Social corrections might work because they communicate how other people view a piece of information, and an individual might use this signal as something to which they align their own assessment of a post. This might be due to the fact that this alignment is a resource-efficient heuristic, or because users want to be in line with others, meaning that a bandwagon effect or norm is at play. This would explain why corrections work even if they originate from unknown others or peers that might not be experts on the topic.

For instance, similar to Vraga and Bode (2017), Badrinathan and Chauchard (2023) refer to credibility of corrections as a reason for their effectiveness, albeit in their view credibility does not derive from the provision of an external source. The starting point for them is that users often see information on complex topics on social media that they might not be familiar with, while having only limited time and cognitive resources to assess what is true and what is false. In this context, corrective comments from others are a heuristic that allow users to make this assessment in a resource efficient manner. Corrections from people whom someone knows personally would be more credible (and thus effective), but corrections could also be seen as credible from unknown sources. Using data from India, Badrinathan and Chauchard (2023) point out that in very large WhatsApp groups, members do not necessarily know each other personally but can still assume that others are like-minded. Thus, strangers would be perceived as (unknown) peers, whose comments are effective because they are still credible corrections. In this way, the proposed mechanism is quite akin to a bandwagon effect, which has been referred to by Colliander (2019) and Boot et al. (2021).

According to Colliander (2019), as well as Boot et al. (2021), social corrections work because individuals want to conform to what they perceive as a majority position of a group. This follows the Asch paradigm (Asch, 1951).

When it comes to opinion formation, research also refers to a bandwagon heuristic (Nadeau et al., 1993). The "bandwagon effect describes how individuals adapt their own opinions to conform to the public's opinions" (Boot et al., 2021, p. 2). Applying the bandwagon effect to social media, one would expect a user to adjust their views to the positions of others who are perceived as peers (Sundar, 2008; Lowe-Calverley & Grieve, 2018; Waddell, 2018a, 2018b). A user does not know where the majority stands on an issue, but likes, comments, and shares can provide the signals about the positions of others that drive the heuristic. However, Boot et al. (2021) eventually conclude that a bandwagon effect is not a likely driver of social corrections' effect.

Recent research has explored how social corrections can convey norms that influence accuracy perceptions. Gimpel et al. (2021) differentiate between the effectiveness of descriptive norms (how most others behave) and injunctive norms (what is socially approved). They found that signaling a descriptive norm alone – that a group of other users flagged a post – was ineffective, but became effective when combined with an injunctive norm (a reminder of how much of a problem misinformation on social media is). Evidence remains mixed regarding the role of norms, possibly also due to differences in operationalizations across studies (Epstein et al., 2021; Gimpel et al., 2021; Prike et al., 2024).

4.1.3 Dissensus Heuristic

On the other hand, some researchers suggest that in the low-effort processing context of social media, indicators of credibility matter less than the mere presence of allegedly disconfirming comments. Anspach and Carlson (2020), for instance, analyze user comments that describe true news posts as factually incorrect. They do not assume that conformity or a bandwagon effect explain why user comments matter. Instead, they suggest that in a situation in which user comments contrast the information displayed in an original post, readers experience a cognitive dissonance (compared to a situation in which comments do not flag a post as inaccurate). As a result, readers "may question the veracity of either piece of information," that is, the accuracy of the original post or the accuracy of comments. The decisive part is that all information will be seen "as less credible than in a situation of consistency" (Anspach & Carlson, 2020, p. 703). While they test this in the context of comments that refute the accuracy of true news, the same mechanism would imply that corrective comments make it less likely for people to believe false news.

4.1.4 Recency Effects

Similarly, comments might also affect users for the mere reason that they are processed after the original information, and the potentially stronger impact that recency effects have. Haugtvedt and Wegener (1994) discuss that information that is processed most recently can have a particularly strong effect on attitudes. Such recency effects are usually associated with low attitude strength, indicating that these effects only play a role if individuals do not have strong preexisting opinions. Recency effects are documented in several domains (Brunel & Nelson, 2003; Abualsaud & Smucker, 2019).

Humans are often considered cognitive misers, meaning that most of their processing tends to be quick and as economical as possible (Kim, Han & Seo, 2020; Stanovich, 2021). While browsing social media, users might not reflect much on every piece of misinformation and each corrective comment encountered, which could make it particularly likely for recency effects to occur (Haugtvedt & Wegener, 1994). Indeed, findings suggest that social media users are more influenced by corrections when they read them after a news post (Cacciatore, 2021; Dai, Yu & Shen, 2021). Dai, Yu and Shen (2021) find that debunking strategies are more effective than prebunking, because recency effects leave the corrections more salient when they are read last. Most of the literature appears to agree that recency effects play some role in misinformation processing (Ecker et al., 2015; Cacciatore, 2021; Dai, Yu & Shen, 2021).

4.2 Social Corrections Help People to Spot False News

We find that social corrections consistently reduce the perceived accuracy of false news and they decrease the intention of users to like and share such posts. We test three types of corrective comment interventions on these outcomes in three countries (see Section 3 for a more extensive discussion of the experimental design). We find statistically significant effects for 25 out of the 29 relationships (Figure 9). Thus, there is a systematic pattern across countries, in the context of a variety of false news stories and different platforms (Instagram, Facebook, and Twitter). The similarity of treatment effects is particularly noteworthy given that we increased the signal strength of the corrective comments in some cases. The pattern that we find suggests that corrections can be effective even when they do not include a source; moreover, an amplified signal does not necessarily lead to a greater effect. These results warrant a closer look, both because this is important to identify best practices and because these results contrast with some prior findings in the literature.

We conducted our fieldwork sequentially, so results and insights from one country could help inform our decisions about what to field in the next country. As a consequence, there are some subtle differences in our experiments across the three national contexts of the UK, Italy, and Germany. To foreground our results across countries, treatments that question the accuracy of the social media post

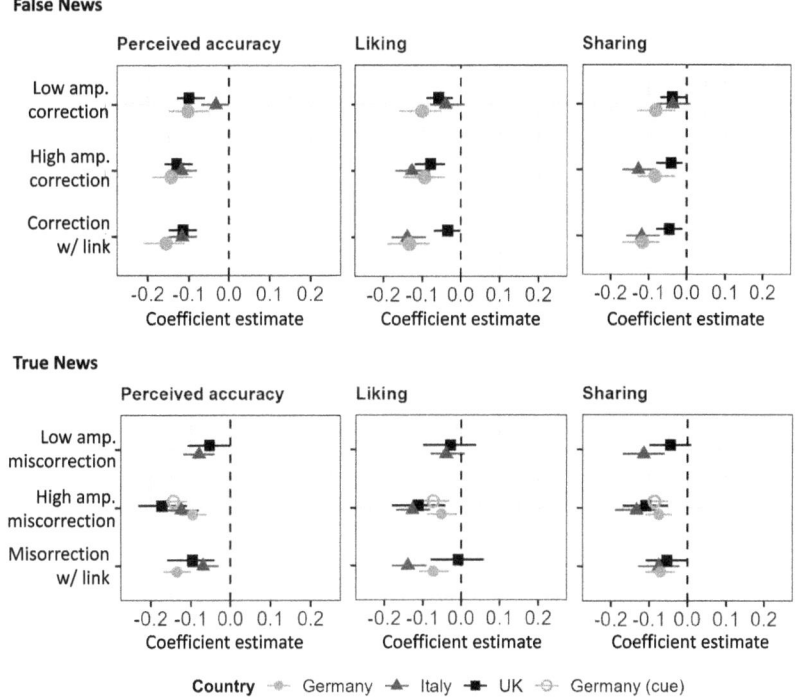

Figure 9 Effects of corrections as well as miscorrections on perceived accuracy, proclivity to like and share false as well as true news.

Note: Circles, squares, and triangles show point estimates. Lines show 95 percent confidence intervals. Multilevel models that control for ideological alignment of the respective post and demographic characteristics of respondents (age, gender, and level of education). Low amp.: low amplification (few likes or comments); high amp.: high amplification (many likes or comments). The corresponding results tables can be found in the online appendix.

almost always decrease both the perceived accuracy of the headline claim as well as the self-reported likelihood to like or share that content. Moreover, there is not a statistically significant difference between the treatments. Put succinctly, social corrections "work." There are, however, two important nuances that accompany this takeaway. First, we use scare quotes because social corrections reduce the perceived accuracy of both false and true content (we expand on this point in Section 4.3). Second, our various manipulations that sought to amplify the strength of the corrective signal (including a justifying link in comment, changing the number of likes for a corrective comment, using two corrective comments) did not noticeably increase the size of the treatment effect.

4.2.1 Attempting to Increase the Strength of the Corrective Signal

Our iterative approach to amplify the strength of the corrective signal, went as follows: In UK fieldwork, we tested the effect of corrective messages that were either not amplified (low amplification), or were amplified because the corrective message received a lot of likes from other users (high amplification). We also tested by including a link to a fact-checking website, which we return to below (compare Lupua & McCubbins, 1998; Nyhan, 2010).

In our surveys in Italy and Germany, we showed more corrective comments. (To increase external validity, we also increased the total number of comments; see the overview of conditions in the online appendix). This use of multiple comments follows the suggestion from the literature that users might not spend the cognitive resources that would be required in order for the number of likes to affect users. Boot et al. (2021) argue that "likes" are not a simple and fast "system 1" heuristic, but rather considering how to interpret the number of likes requires "system 2" thinking to produce effects. We find the low amplification condition (i.e., only one corrective user comment) to have a statistically significant negative effect on all three outcomes in Germany but not in Italy. The high amplification condition (several corrective comments) has a statistically significant negative effect on all outcomes in Germany and in Italy. Thus, a stronger signal (more corrective comments rather than just one corrective comment) consistently shows a significant effect across the full set of outcomes. However, the difference between the various amplification conditions is not itself significant, consistent with Gelman and Stern (2006).

As mentioned above, we also tested a further amplification strategy in all three countries by sometimes including a link to a fact-check as part of the corrective comment. Conditions with a link consistently have significant negative effects across outcomes and countries. However, the inclusion of a link does not *increase* the magnitude of the corrective effect. Including a link to a fact-check does not seem to amplify the strength of the corrective signal.

4.2.2 Ideological Alignment

One contributing factor to falling for misinformation is that people are biased toward accepting claims that are ideologically aligned to their world view or ideological orientation as true, even when the information is false (Flynn et al., 2017). Typically, this pattern is attributed to directionally motivated reasoning with differential application of cognitive effort to scrutinize the truth value of claims that are either worldview consistent or inconsistent. Importantly, recent research has suggested that a directionally motivated reasoning approach is observationally equivalent to either other motivations in the broader motivated reasoning framework (Bayes & Druckman, 2021) or to a Bayesian approach (Little, 2021).

Accordingly, we test the role of social corrections in the context of ideologically aligned and not-aligned misinformation. Our surveys included measures that allow us to determine whether information is and is not ideologically aligned: For instance, we measure how respondents view vaccines, science, 5G network technology, Russia's attack on Ukraine, and so on, before respondents enter the experimental part of the survey. This way, we can identify when a social media post is ideologically aligned and when a correction is not aligned for a respondent. In line with the literature, we find that individuals are more likely to believe false news posts that are in line with their world views (see Section 2). For instance, individuals who do not trust vaccines are more likely to believe false news stories about vaccines.

In this section we are specifically interested in whether social corrections help individuals to identify false content even when it is not ideologically aligned. Conducting this analysis goes beyond our preregistration (see Stoeckel et al. (2024) for results executed as preregistered). We account for ideological alignment in two ways. First, our results control for ideological alignment, using a dummy that indicates for each observation whether its content is ideologically aligned for a respondent. Thus, the results discussed above and in Figure 9 control for ideological alignment.

Second, we interact all treatment effects with the dummy variables that indicate whether content is ideologically aligned. The respective marginal effect plots (Figure 10) show treatment effects for the case of ideologically aligned and not-aligned content. Consistent with the emerging literature questioning the ubiquity of heterogenous treatment effects due to directionally motivated reasoning (Wood & Porter, 2019; Carey et al., 2022; Coppock, 2023), we find the effects of social corrections are not moderated by prior attitudes in most of our conditions across the three countries. The only exception is the low amplification correction condition in Italy (where the correction is not statistically significant in the case of information that is not ideologically aligned). We conclude that the effect of social corrections does not depend on the ideological alignment of the topic. While directionally motivated reasoning might explain different levels of belief in the first place, it does not seem to affect the extent to which social corrections change underlying beliefs.

4.3 Social Miscorrections Mislead

User comments seem to help against false and misleading information shared on social media. However, if these social corrections are effective against false or misleading content *and* if the effects are not moderated by prior attitudes, might

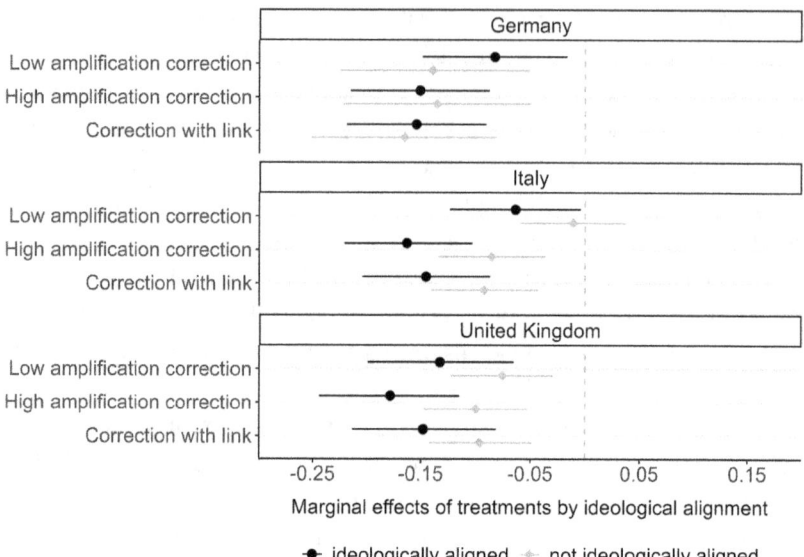

Figure 10 Marginal effects of corrections by ideological alignment and by country (false news).

Note: Results based on an interaction of treatments with ideological alignment dummies. Model specifications are similar to those of the main models shown in Figure 9. Multilevel regressions run separately for each country. Dots show point estimates of marginal effects and lines show a 95 percent confidence interval. Negative marginal effects imply that a respective treatment condition decreases perceived accuracy. This means that a respective (false news) post is perceived as less accurate in the treatment condition compared to a control condition which does not include a correction.

there also be a dark side? Can (inaccurate) user corrections decrease the perceived accuracy of true claims from mainstream news sources?

As shown in Section 2, a significant share of people also mistake true news for false news – suggesting there is scope for user comments to nudge people toward not believing accurate claims. Indeed, we find substantial variation across the stimuli used in our fieldwork: While one of our true news posts was only considered inaccurate by 15 percent of respondents, three posts were considered inaccurate by more than half of the sample that saw them. What happens if other social media users post comments which say that these true news stories are in fact inaccurate? We call these misleading comments *miscorrections* and examine their effect on accuracy perceptions as well as engagement intent (liking and sharing).

Examining the role of comments in the context of true news is important because far more news shared on social media is true (Acerbi et al., 2022). Some studies already point toward the problematic effects of miscorrections in the context of true news. For instance, Anspach and Carlson (2020) examine the role of miscorrections in the context of social media posts about Donald Trump, and find that miscorrective comments are more likely to be remembered. Based on a North American student sample, Vraga and Bode (2022) find miscorrections to decrease perceived accuracy of true news in the context of health information.

If miscorrections leave an imprint on social media users, misinformation comes not only in the form of false news but also results from factually incorrect commentary from other users. Over the longer term, miscorrections might contribute to a more general reduction in trust in information, making it more difficult for people to decide what is true and what is false.

We test the effect of miscorrections using a design that parallels our examination of social corrections on false content. Our experiments use the true news material shown in Section 2 and test how miscorrections affect perceived accuracy as well as intentions to like and share a post. In our fieldwork in the UK and in Italy, the different experimental conditions for *miscorrections* mirror those for corrections. In the UK, we use a control condition without any corrective comments plus three miscorrection conditions: a low amplification condition with two user comments (one being a miscorrection with a small number of likes), a high amplification condition where more than 100 users like the miscorrective comment, and a miscorrection that additionally includes a link to a fact-checking website. In Italy, amplification means a greater number of miscorrective comments, rather than more likes. The low amplification treatment condition includes just one miscorrective comment (besides one other non-corrective comment). The high amplification conditions include three miscorrections from users (among a fourth comment). The last condition includes again a link to a website that seemingly bolsters the miscorrective comment of a user.

The results show that miscorrections affect accuracy perceptions of true news (Figure 9). All but one of our treatment conditions reduce the perceived accuracy of true news compared to the control condition (the lone nonsignificant condition was the low amplification condition in the UK, $p < 0.07$). Social miscorrections also decrease the intentions of respondents to like and share the true social media posts that they see, albeit the pattern is more mixed (while all treatment conditions are statistically significant in Italy, only one of the three treatment conditions is statistically significant in the UK).

Turning now to differences across our treatments and different forms of amplifying the *mis*corrective message of the comment, results are strikingly similar to those we found for corrections of false news. For instance, miscorrections that include a link to a website which seemingly bolsters the comment are no stronger than comments without a link. Our Italian fieldwork also shows that additional miscorrections do not have a stronger effect than just a single miscorrective comment. These findings are important to note as, in the case of true news, it shows just how easily perceptions of true news can be affected by user commentary.

We also conduct an additional analysis (not preregistered) that tests whether the effect of miscorrections depends on the ideological alignment of the news content (Figure 11). We find that miscorrections affect accuracy perceptions of true news irrespective of ideological alignment in Germany. In Italy, we find that miscorrections affect accuracy perceptions of ideological aligned true information consistently, but they do not consistently affect perceptions of true posts that are not ideologically aligned. In contrast, in the UK, miscorrection consistently affects accuracy perceptions of posts that are not ideologically aligned, but they do not affect perceptions of ideologically aligned true information. One should note that content of posts differs between countries. Hence, rather than taking these results as manifestations of country differences, they can result from the particular content that was used. In sum, miscorrections have the ability to affect accuracy perceptions of true news and this can happen in the context of information that is ideologically aligned and when information is not ideologically aligned. Future research could examine the precise role of ideological alignment in this context.

4.4 Role of Source Cues

Is it possible that some media organizations have sufficient standing and credibility that they are not subject to miscorrection effects? Clear source cues from respected media institutions have the potential to protect against miscorrections, just as source cues from untrustworthy sites may do the opposite. Indeed, how social media platforms choose to display content from news sites is an important decision. (X, formerly Twitter, made the decision to stop displaying headlines in people's feeds to links from news sites.) To help answer this question, we examine whether the inclusion or absence of a source cue or news outlet logo affects the perceived accuracy of the headline claim.

Accurate news stories might be posted by social media users without showing or linking to a source. However, legitimate news stories are often broken first by professional media outlets. When social media users share this content, other

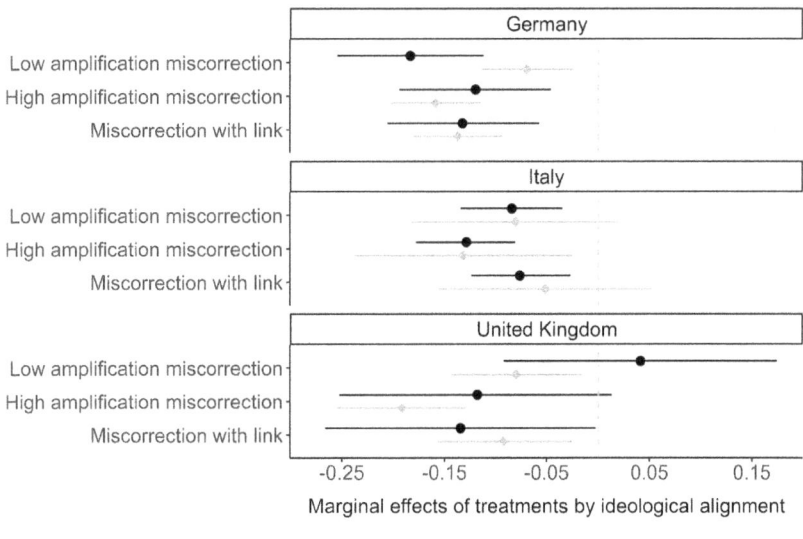

Figure 11 Marginal effects of miscorrections by ideological alignment and by country (true news).

Note: Results based on an interaction of treatments with ideological alignment dummies. Model specifications are similar to those of the main models shown in Figure 9. Multilevel regressions run separately for each country with observations nested within individuals. Dots show point estimates of marginal effects and lines show a 95 percent confidence interval. Negative marginal effects imply that a respective treatment condition decreases perceived accuracy. This means that a respective (true news) post is perceived as less accurate in the treatment condition compared to a control condition that does not include a miscorrection.

people might thus see a source cue – that is, a logo or name of a news outlet. News from media outlets could be inaccurate as well, but a logo could be a strong signal indicating that a piece of information has been produced or vetted by professionals (assuming that the logo has not been added in a malicious way). Our results show that miscorrections decrease the perceived accuracy of true news posts as well as the intention to like or share a true news post even when source cues are displayed (Figure 9, bottom panel, parameter estimates for "Germany cue").

The literature is mixed when it comes to the role of source cues. Several studies find evidence of source credibility having a significant effect on accuracy perceptions (Swire et al., 2017; Nadarevic et al., 2020; Traberg & van der Linden, 2022), but the results are inconsistent (e.g., Clayton et al., 2019; Dias, Pennycook & Rand, 2020; Baum & Abdel Rahman, 2021).

Figure 12 Example of a social media post with source cue in the upper left corner (true news; source cue refers to the German newspaper Süddeutsche Zeitung). Translated content (from German): The autumn wave hits hospitals with full force. Top user comment: Now they start again to tell fairy tales. Everyone knows by now that there was no overcrowding in the health system. Bottom comment: That was bound to happen.

In the true news part of the German fieldwork, we deviate from the pattern used in other countries and for false news in Germany (i.e., we do not show a low amplification condition, a high amplification condition, and a correction with link condition). Respondents are randomly assigned to seeing either the control condition (no comment, no source cue), a high amplification condition with source cue (source cue shown as part of the original post, several miscorrective comments), the same condition without source cue, or a miscorrection with link. The different true news posts include a variety of news outlet labels, most of them being highly reputable mainstream outlets (e.g., tagesschau, FAZ, NDR Info; see Figure 12 and Figure 13 as well as our treatment material on OSF). The results for the treatment condition with these source cues are substantively similar to the ones of the treatment condition that

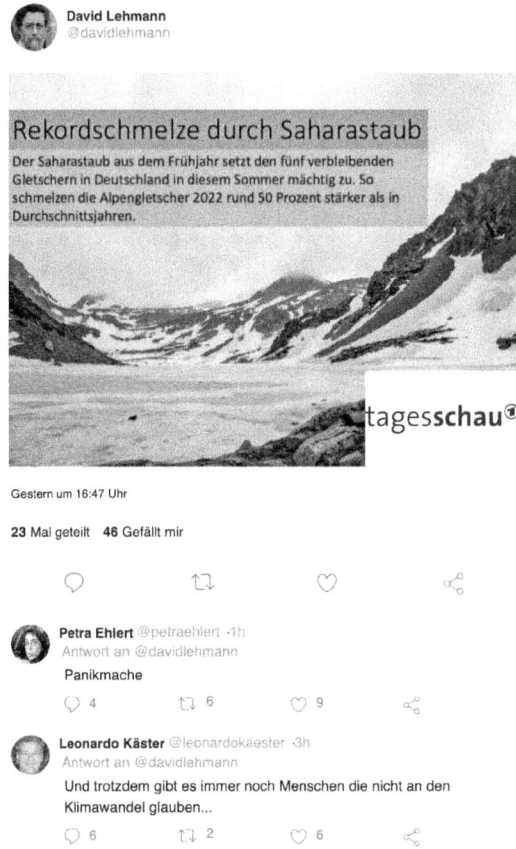

Figure 13 Example of a social media post that shows a source cue in the bottom right corner (true news; source cue refers to the German news broadcast tagesschau). Headline: Record melting due to Sahara dust. Top comment: Fearmongering. Bottom comment: And yet there are people who do not believe in climate change.

shows the same treatments without source cues. We do not find that a source cue for the true news makes miscorrections less effective. Respondents perceive a lower accuracy when misleading comments tag a post as false whether the original post includes a source cue or not (bottom panel, Figure 9).

4.5 Heterogeneous Treatment Effects

In Section 2, we found that anti-expert sentiments, susceptibility to social influence, and cognitive reflection capabilities are related to the ability of individuals to identify false and true news. Do these individual differences play a role in the effectiveness of social corrections? In other words, having observed a direct effect from these variables, we now also examine whether they have a moderating effect on our treatments. We test this possibility by interacting our treatments with these three variables, and we examine the interaction effects for all three outcomes in all three countries: accuracy perceptions, intention to like, and the intention to share false news posts. Our sample is well powered to detect interaction effects (see Section 3 for details on the simulation-based approach we used to estimate the power needed). However, while there are statistically significant interactions between some individual characteristics in some countries, we do not find a consistent pattern that holds across treatments and across countries.

For instance, individuals with more pronounced anti-expert positions are more likely to believe false news (Section 2). While individuals with such positions might be unlikely to take cues from mainstream media outlets or professional fact-checkers that correct falsehoods (Lyons et al., 2021), they could be more likely to accept corrections from other (non-elite) members of the public. Alternatively, anyone who posts corrections could be seen as someone who seeks to take a position of authority from the perspective of a user who trusts their own position as much (or more so) than cues from others. We find a statistically significant interaction in the UK (corrections have a stronger effect among those scoring lower on our anti-expert sentiment measure). The pattern we find in the UK is neither supported by the results from Italy nor by those from Germany, where we do not find any statistically significant interactions (Figure 14).

In line with the literature, we also find cognitive reflection skills to be related to false news susceptibility in Section 2. There are several potential reasons why individuals who score higher on CRT are better able to spot what is likely to be false, one of them being that higher CRT scores are related to individuals processing information they see more thoroughly and in a more critical way. The same cognitive process could mean that those high in CRT are processing also comments – and thus social corrections – more systematically, which in turn would render corrections more effective. While two interaction are statistically significant, the overall pattern does not support the notion that treatment effects are conditional on CRT scores (Figure 15). This null finding is a very important one as it sheds some light on the role of information processing for the effect of social corrections. Apparently, individuals who score low and high in CRT are affected in a rather similar way by social corrections. We interpret this as evidence that the very reason why social corrections affect users is not because they process the corrections very thoroughly (if that was the case, we would expect effects to be more pronounced among those who are predisposed to process information more thoroughly).

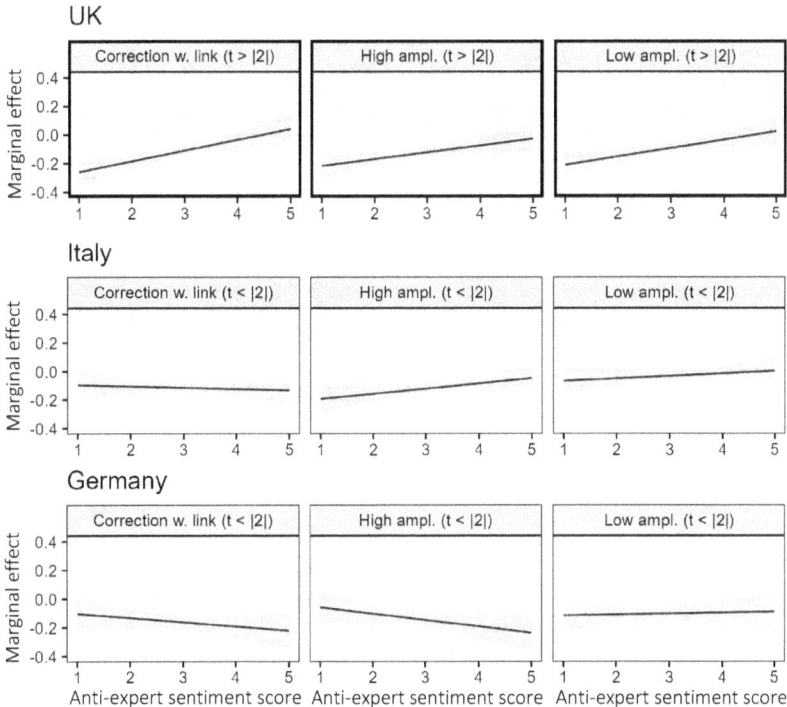

Figure 14 Correction effects in the context of false news by levels of anti-expert sentiment scores across the UK, Italy, and Germany. Each graph shows the marginal effect of the respective treatment (i.e. low amplification, high amplification, amplification with link condition) by levels of anti-expert sentiment. The outcome is accuracy perceptions of false news. Grey shading around lines show the 95 percent confidence interval. Bold frames indicate statistically significant interaction effects. Results from multilevel models. Corrections have a stronger effect among individuals with lower levels of anti-expert sentiments in the UK.

The third individual level characteristic we take into account is susceptibility to social influence. As shown in Section 2, individuals who are more susceptible to social influence are more likely to believe false news and at the same time also more likely to believe true news. Analyzing the interaction between the effect of social corrections and variation in susceptibility to social influence can give us important insights on the mechanism that explains why corrections work in the first place. One set of studies (e.g., Colliander 2019; Boot et al., 2021) points toward a bandwagon effect and, in a similar vein, to conformity as a reason why corrective comments might have an effect on citizens. A key part of

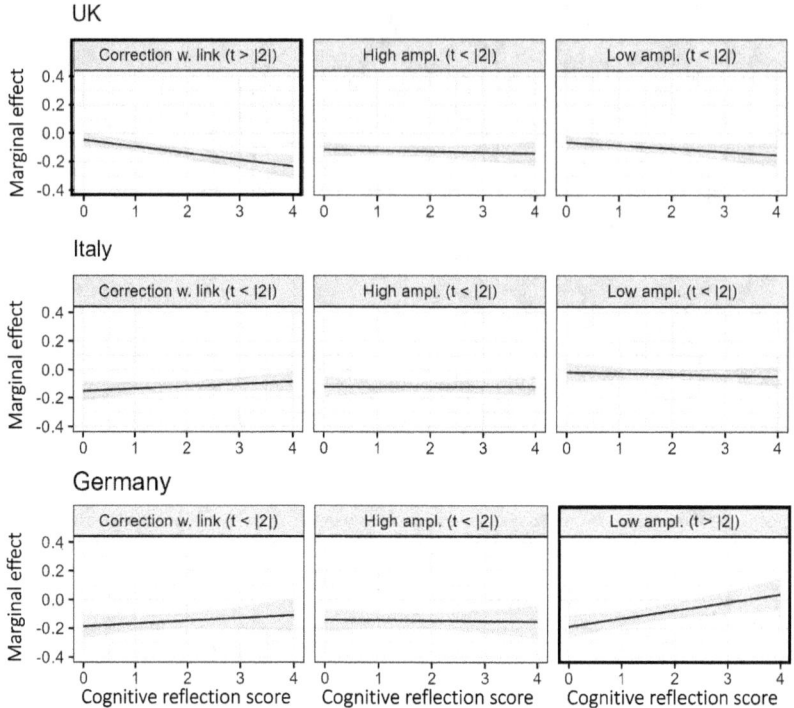

Figure 15 Correction effects in the context of false news by levels of cognitive reflection scores across the UK, Italy, and Germany. Each graph shows the marginal effect of the respective correction effect (i.e. low amplification, high amplification, amplification with link condition) by levels of CRT-score. The outcome is accuracy perceptions of false news. Grey shading around lines show the 95 percent confidence interval. A bold frame indicates a statistically significant interaction effect. Results from multilevel models.

that mechanism is that individuals adjust their views or behavior to those of others. Susceptibility to social influence is about individual differences in the extent to which individuals react to other people. Hence, if conformity is a reason why social corrections work, we would assume the corrections to have a stronger effect among individuals who are more susceptible to social influence. What we find is a mixed picture. There is a statistically significant relationship in the UK and for some conditions also in Italy (Figure 16). However, the effect of corrections seems to be stronger among individuals who are less susceptible to social influence (rather than more susceptible). There is no evidence of an interaction in Germany. In sum, we do not find that susceptibility to social influence consistently conditions the effect of social corrections. This casts

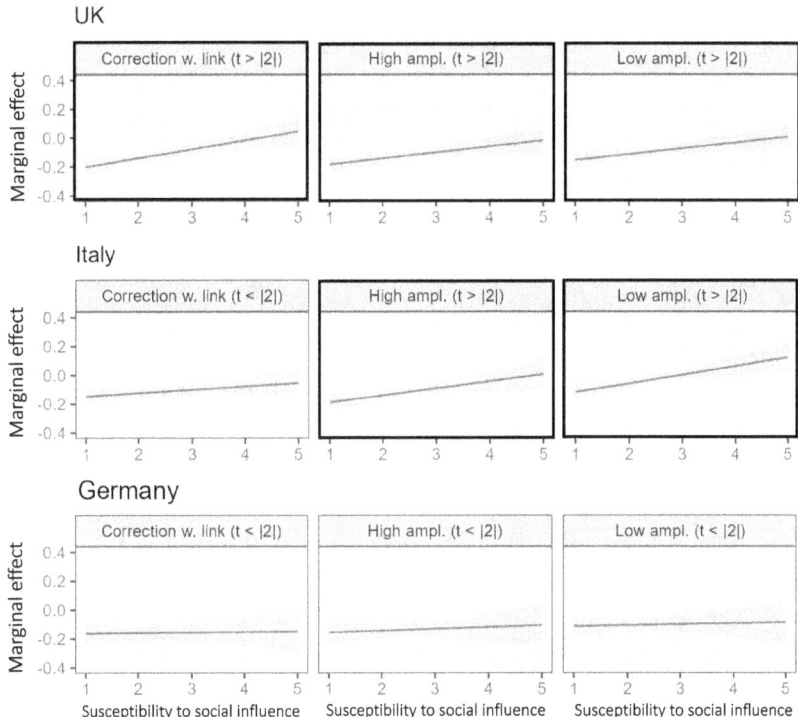

Figure 16 Correction effects in the context of false news by levels of susceptibility to social influence across the UK, Italy, and Germany. Each graph shows the marginal effect of the respective correction effect (i.e. low amplification, high amplification, amplification with link condition) by levels of susceptibility to social influence. The outcome is accuracy perceptions of false news. The top panel refers to the UK, the middle one to Italy, and the bottom one to Germany. Grey shading around lines show the 95 percent confidence interval. A bold frame indicates statistically significant interaction effects. Results from multilevel models. Corrections have a stronger effect among individuals with lower susceptibility to social influence in the UK and in two of the conditions in Italy.

doubt on the idea that conformity is a reason why social corrections have an impact on user perceptions of accuracy. That is because we would expect individuals who are more likely to adjust their views to others to react more strongly to social corrections, but this is not what we find.

We also tested whether individual differences in anti-expert sentiments, cognitive reflection skills, and susceptibility to social influence condition the influence of miscorrections. As was the case with corrections, we do not observe a consistent pattern of interactions (we observe mostly null effects). Miscorrective commentary seems to affect individuals in a similar fashion irrespective of these differences.

4.6 Limitations

We want to highlight several important limitations. First, and most importantly, we do not measure the effect of corrective comments in real life social media feeds. Though, it is not clear that it would be possible to run a study that embedded randomized user corrections into people's social media feeds. While there are several factors that give us lots of confidence in the robustness of findings – the large number of observations, replicating findings across countries, and getting consistent results across different stimuli and treatments – we are always subject to the fact that data were recorded in the artificial context of a study. While the social media posts that we showed respondents follow the design of Twitter, Instagram, or Facebook, respondents did not see this information in a context of a feed with information from friends as well as strangers. The fact that the social media posts were not created or posted by friends should not, on its own, be a major concern. First, this is a very common experience on social media sites, where users often are exposed to and interact with those outside their offline network. As mentioned above, we also believe that this leads to more conservative effect estimates, because users would likely be expected to pay more attention to corrections from friends.

Another limitation is that participants were rating the accuracy of shorter statements rather than full articles and they could not access a full article if they would have wanted to (e.g., to better assess the accuracy of the headline). Here, we are following not only a common approach in social media misinformation research, where only showing headlines is a common procedure (Pennycook et al., 2021). Social media users are in fact often – or even most of the time – making decisions, for instance to share a post, just based on the headline. From that point of view, one might argue that reducing the extent to which people are sharing content just based on a headline should be the goal of an intervention. Additionally, individuals who would like to see a full story before feeling comfortable enough to assess the accuracy of a piece of information or before sharing a post might in fact not be the group of people most susceptible to misinformation (e.g., people scoring higher on cognitive reflection – i.e., those who are predisposed to reflect more before making a decision – are less susceptible to misinformation).

Another limitation is that asking respondents about accuracy, liking, and sharing as we do creates an artificial situation that does not fully resemble real social media feeds. Asking respondents about these three outcomes might affect both accuracy perceptions and sharing intentions (see Epstein et al., 2023, and our discussion about that point in Section 3). We have confidence in our results because of the robust pattern across posts and countries. Yet, we kept asking these outcomes in all fieldwork, and hence all measures are potentially affected by this. However, sharing is a salient feature of social media and therefore conducting our study without asking about sharing intentions would not have increased external validity from our perspective (and removing accuracy perception was not an option, given that this is our main outcome). We appreciate, however, that this is an important issue and limitation that deserves attention in future work.

Finally, our results might be driven by the particular material that we used: the content of the post, the way corrections were written, and the way miscorrections were written. As Section 2 shows nicely, content matters – some content is more believable than other content. In a similar vein, corrections or miscorrections might just be more effective in some contexts than in others. However, we show robustness by covering a particularly wide set of topics as well as a wide set of (mis)corrective comments. Corrections (and miscorrections) seem to work on average.

4.7 Conclusion

In this section, we show that social corrections of false news seem to help people identify inaccurate information from social media. One of the main reasons why individuals believe that something is true even though it is false is because a piece of information is ideologically aligned – that is, it is in line with ideological orientations or prior attitudes. We find that, on average, the effects in our experiments are not conditional on ideological alignment. However, while this is an important result, its effect should not be taken out of proportion: Motivated reasoning and the role of partisanship are strong forces, and the precise effect of them – relative to social corrections – is likely to depend much on the specific piece of misinformation and how strong someone's opinion is on an issue or whether the topic is central to someone's identity. Put differently, we would not expect a vaccine opponent to see a (false) social media post claiming that vaccines are ineffective differently just because other users are posting corrective information.

We tested several versions of corrective comments as well as how variation in likes and the number of corrective comments affect readers. We find that the mere presence of a correction is more important than the number of comments or likes (that a corrective comment received). Just because likes and fact checks do not strengthen the effects of corrections, one should not dismiss them as irrelevant – likes may matter in order for a corrective comment to be salient and fact checks could help writers to be sure that they are in fact correcting accurately. We return to their important role in a part on best practices in Section 6 of this Element.

Our findings also shed light on the mechanism that drives the effect of social corrections. Our experiment focuses on the role of corrections posted by strangers, rather than corrections from friends or family. Signals from friends and family might likely be more effective and thus what we observe is likely a conservative estimate of correction effects. Yet, the reason why corrections work might not in fact result from commenters who are perceived as credible or because users might want to conform to the views of the general public. Rather, information processing might be much less systematic, and because information is processed with few cognitive resources, recency effects can dominate. Meaning, a correction or refutation would work merely because it casts doubt on a piece of information that has just been seen – that is, because doubts are raised briefly after an original piece of information has been processed.

Other patterns of our results point in a similar direction. For instance, if source credibility would be very important, corrections with a link or those reinforced by several individuals (by likes or by people who agree) could be expected to have a stronger effect, but this is not what we find. If conformity considerations (i.e., bandwagon effects) were central, then individuals who are more susceptible to social influence could be expected to respond more to the signals from others. We do not find this interaction effect either. We also do not find corrections to have a stronger effect among those who are predisposed to process information in a more reflective manner, even though we find cognitive reflection skills to help people generally to identify false information (see Section 2). Thus, in sum, our results do not support the idea that conformity, credibility considerations, or a particularly thorough processing of comments is the mechanism through which corrective comments affect users. Instead, individuals are more likely to process information in a less thorough way, which is why the piece of information considered after an initial post – a set of refutations – might affect user perceptions. For this very reason, though, miscorrections appear to be equally effective at casting doubt.

5 Who Writes Comments?

Social corrections are low cost in that they rely on organic engagement habits among the public, but engaging in corrections is not necessarily a costless activity for social media users. There are numerous factors that may cause cognitive friction for would-be commenters. This friction may not be equally distributed across the public, leaving open the question of who habitually comments and whether this behavior is correlated with the ability to discern true from false news. In other words, in addition to investigating whether comments affect perceived veracity, it is important to know how the public feels about engaging in corrective action (and whether, given the opportunity, they actually *engage* in social correction). It is likewise essential to identify how these feelings about engagement vary across the population (i.e., whether some groups are more likely to engage in corrective action). To better our understanding of these questions, we fielded a population-based survey in Germany with nearly 3,800 respondents in February 2023, which sheds light on public perceptions of user comments on social media. We selected Germany out of the three countries we focus on in the rest of the Element because it received less attention in the literature on misinformation than the UK while levels of populism are less pronounced than in Italy (in that sense, Italy would be more of an extreme case rather than a representative one). The survey reflects the German population with regard to age, gender, education, and region. The question wordings for each measure discussed below can be found in the online appendix.

5.1 What Do Social Media Users Do When They See Misinformation?

Taking time to correct others online might impose personal costs since it requires effort (Druckman, 2022). It also may hurt relationships (Bode, 2016; Yang et al., 2017; Gurgun et al., 2023) and some may prefer to avoid conflict (Chadwick et al., 2023). Similarly, correcting others may go against behavioral norms (Gurgun et al., 2023) or conflict with one's personality characteristics (e.g., high self-esteem is linked to a lower likelihood of denouncing false content shared by strangers; Johnson & Kromka, 2023). As such, there are numerous reasons as to why many members of the public may avoid corrective behavior.

Toward this end, our survey asked respondents about their typical reactions when they encounter information on social media that they find inaccurate. Based on the self-reports in the survey, the most common behavior is for people to disregard such information (61 percent report that they ignore false news often or most of the time). The second most frequent reaction for users is to unfollow or unfriend the person who posted misinformation (48 percent do this often or most of the time), followed by flagging misinformation to the platform (26 percent). Approximately one in five (21 percent) respondents say that they react to misinformation by writing corrective comments often or most of the time. In sum, a majority say they take an avoidance tactic, though a sizable minority are frequent correctors.

5.2 Who Is Responsible for Fixing the Problem?

Aside from interpersonal reasons, individuals might refrain from commenting because of their views about the problem of misinformation itself – that is, who is responsible, and whether social corrections are a valid means to address it. Some may view individual action as less preferable to top-down action by platforms or governments (Cheng & Luo, 2020; Tully et al., 2022). Others may eschew corrective action if they think it may inadvertently amplify misinformation (Swire et al., 2017).

Our survey finds that users have a clear ranking in mind when it comes to the role that social media companies, users, and governments should play when it comes to fighting misinformation. Our German sample seems to primarily allocate responsibility for dealing with misinformation to social media companies, rather than government. Over half (63 percent) of respondents say that companies play a big role in this regard, while about a third (37 percent) believe that companies play a small or no role. When it comes to users, 56 percent say they should play a key role, versus just 44 percent who say they should play a small or no role. Finally, according to almost half of respondents (48 percent), governments should take on a major role to combat misinformation. This clearly outweighs the approximately 14 percent who oppose any government interference in this domain.

Reacting to misinformation poses a potential quandary for social media users inclined to take action. Social media algorithms typically upweight content that receives significant engagement. By commenting or interacting with untrustworthy content (with the purpose of trying to correct it), users might inadvertently make misinformation more salient to others. Thus, people might avoid interacting with misinformation specifically to stop spreading it.

The degree of the correction/salience tradeoff depends on the algorithm of a social media platform – what is promoted and how much interaction triggers this (which individual users are extremely unlikely to have direct knowledge about). However, people might have a preference regarding the world they would prefer to live in, which gives us an insight into their thinking about the trade-off between corrections and lack of salience. Users could prefer a situation where misinformation is corrected even at the price of salience, or one where it is not corrected and misinformation less salient. As can be read from Table 2, 73 percent of our survey respondents prefer misinformation to be corrected even if corrections contribute to salience.

Table 2 Priority of corrections at the price of salience

"Do you find it more important that false information is corrected or that false information is seen by less people?"	
Prefer limiting spread	Prefer corrections
27.1	72.9

Note: Table shows percentages. Authors' data. Survey fielded in Germany in February 2023 with population quotas on gender, age, education, and region. $N = 3{,}792$.

5.3 Views on the Efficacy and Value of Corrections

Even though most seem to accept the salience trade-off raised by corrective actions, social corrections themselves could be seen as ineffective or futile (Lyons, 2022b; Gurgun et al., 2023). However, most people do not seem to view corrective comments as ineffective. We find that a majority (73 percent) of respondents believe that corrections of false news on social media help against the spread of misinformation. In a similar vein, most people (76 percent) think that the collective efforts of users could make a difference in the fight against misinformation.

A large share of respondents also believes that they personally are able to correct inaccurate information (73 percent). We can also map confidence against correction frequency, which can be seen in Table 3. Only about 23 percent of those with confidence in their ability to correct misinformation actually do so often or most of the time when they see misinformation. This percentage may seem small, but the baseline in the sample for writing corrections is generally low. Therefore, it is potentially concerning that among those who do not feel confident to correct misinformation, 15 percent still state that they react to misinformation by writing a corrective comment frequently or most of the time.

Along these lines, it is also important to consider views toward miscorrections and their perceived effects on oneself and others. As we show in Section 4, comments which wrongly attack the veracity of true headlines decrease perceived accuracy, complicating decision-making about what is true news and what is false news. Our survey investigates whether this is a concern people have about comments that other users post on social media. Indeed, we find that 76 percent of respondents believe that user comments can make it more difficult for people to identify true and false news. Consistent with other research (Sun et al., 2008), people are, however, more worried about others being affected by inaccurate corrections than about themselves. Only 50 percent of respondents also fear that comments might make it more difficult for themselves to identify

Table 3 Proportion of respondents writing social corrections by subjective ability to correct misinformation

		Self-reported correction frequency		
		Never, rarely	Often, most of the time	
Subjective ability to correct false online content	Low	85.0	15.0	100
	High	76.5	23.5	100

Note: Table shows percentages. Authors' data. Survey fielded in Germany in February 2023 with population quotas on gender, age, education, and region. Subjective ability to correct false online content ($N = 3,361$): "In most situations, I am able to correct false information." Disagree completely, disagree somewhat = Low, agree somewhat, agree completely = High. Self-reported correction frequency ($N = 3,763$): respondents were asked "What do you do when you see false information on social media?" For each of six behaviors, we asked about the frequency at which this occurs. Table above refers to "writing comments and saying what was false."

false and true news. Prior work suggests this perceptual gap reflects at least some degree of overconfidence (Lyons et al., 2021; Lyons 2022b).

This can pose a more general problem for social corrections. The high number of people who say that they can largely correct misinformation should be treated with caution: While individuals might have confidence in their ability to correct false news, at least a share of them might overestimate their ability to identify true and false news. Lyons et al. (2021) show that overconfidence is in fact very common. Thus, when people try to correct something they assume to be false even though it is in fact true, they might contribute to the spread of misinformation. For this reason, we now turn to an analysis of commenters' personal characteristics.

5.4 Characteristics of Users Who Write Comments

It is essential to understand potential asymmetries in who tends to comment most often, given the double-edged nature of comments. In our study (Section 4), we find miscorrections to be just as influential as corrections, so examining the relative frequency of each is important for future work (see Metzger et al., 2021). One way we can begin to shed light on this, though indirectly, is to examine the background characteristics of habitual commenters. This may illuminate whether most comments tend to be done by skilled individuals or those less equipped to "get it right" (Trepte & Scherer, 2010; Weeks et al., 2017).

Using our survey where respondents self-report on whether they write corrective comments, we can identify the characteristics of individuals who engage in social corrections more often. To do this, we use data from the survey that we fielded in Germany in February 2023. This survey asks respondents how they typically react when they come across false information on social media. We are particularly interested in the frequency of certain reactions. Thus, for each of six reactions, we ask how frequently this occurs (never, rarely, often, most of the time). The reactions include writing comments that correct inaccurate information, as well as ignoring wrong information, notifying the platform, unfriending the person who posted the information, and so on. For our analysis in this section, we use the data about the frequency with which respondents react to (seemingly) wrong information by posting a correcting comment. As mentioned in Section 5.1, only 21 percent of respondents say that they write comments often or most of the time.

To identify the characteristics that are associated with more frequent commenting, we run an OLS regression. The range of the outcome is 1 to 4 (self-reported frequency: never, rarely, often, most of the time). We regress the frequency with which respondents claim to write comments on a set of demographic variables, measures for political orientations, and attitudinal variables. Figure 17 shows the results.

We first find that views toward corrections matter. Individuals who prioritize corrections over a low salience for misinformation write comments more frequently, as do those who believe that comments can help against the spread of misinformation. We also find that users over 35 write comments less often, while education plays no role. Additionally, we find men to write corrections more frequently, in line with Peacock and Van Duyn (2023), who found that while women are more likely to read comments, men are more frequently the ones writing them. Individuals with higher cognitive reflection test (CRT) scores write comments less often. This specific finding is particularly interesting because some have interpreted CRT as, at least in part, a measure of (cognitive) effort (Pennycook & Rand, 2019b). So, this form of (cognitive) effort does not translate into self-reported effort in another domain. Party affiliation is not related to comment writing frequency, except that those who do not feel close to any party write comments less frequently than all other respondents. Finally, individuals who score higher on an anti-expert measure write comments more frequently, which is a concerning finding given the harm done by miscorrections. Comparing men and women across the different variables, we do not find any significant differences.

We now focus on the confidence that people have in their ability to correct misinformation (Figure 18). Men have more confidence in their ability to correct than women. Yet, gender does not have moderating effects for the other variables

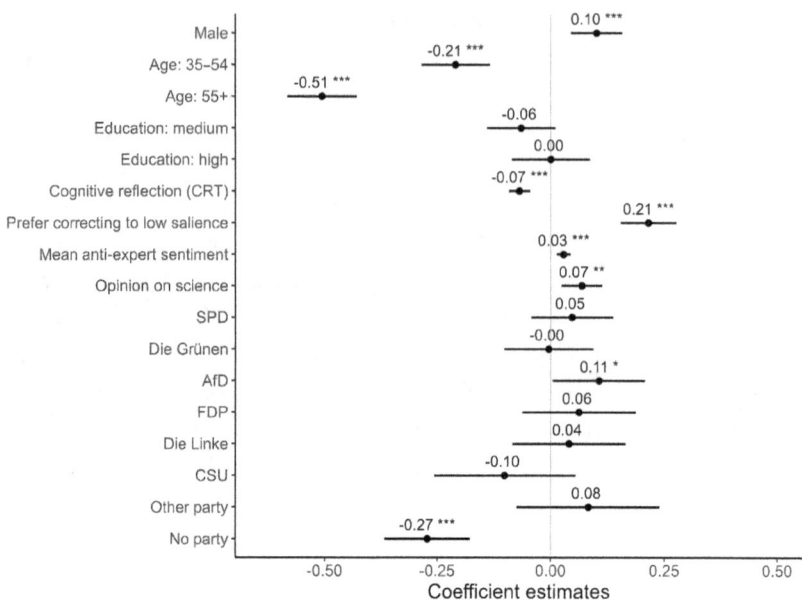

Figure 17 Determinants of correction frequency in response to false social media content.

Note: Measures used above are self-reports. Survey question: "What do you do when you see false information on social media?" For each of six reactions, we ask how frequently it occurs. The dependent variable of the model plotted above is how frequently respondents say that they react by doing the following: "Write a comment and say what was wrong" (never, rarely, often, most of the time). OLS regression, $N = 3,775$. Dots: point estimates, lines: 95 percent confidence interval. SPD: Social Democrats, Die Grünen: Green Party, AfD: Alternative for Germany, FDP: Liberal Party, Die Linke: Left Party, CSU: Bavarian part of Conservative Party. Reference groups: age under 35, female, education: low, party: Conservative (CDU), respondent prefers low salience over corrections of false information. Opinion on science: negative, rather negative, rather positive, positive. CRT: higher values represent higher cognitive reflection test (CRT) capabilities. Anti-expert sentiment score: higher values indicate greater anti-expert sentiment (index consisting of three items; see online appendix). Statistical significance: *($p < 0.05 = *$, $p < 0.01 = **$, $p < 0.001 = ***$)

(tested in a separate analysis). Both individuals with anti-expert positions and positive views toward science feel more confident in their ability to correct. Put differently, those who see science negatively have less confidence in their ability to correct, though this is of course occurring when holding anti-expert positions constant. As with willingness to write comments, education is not significant.

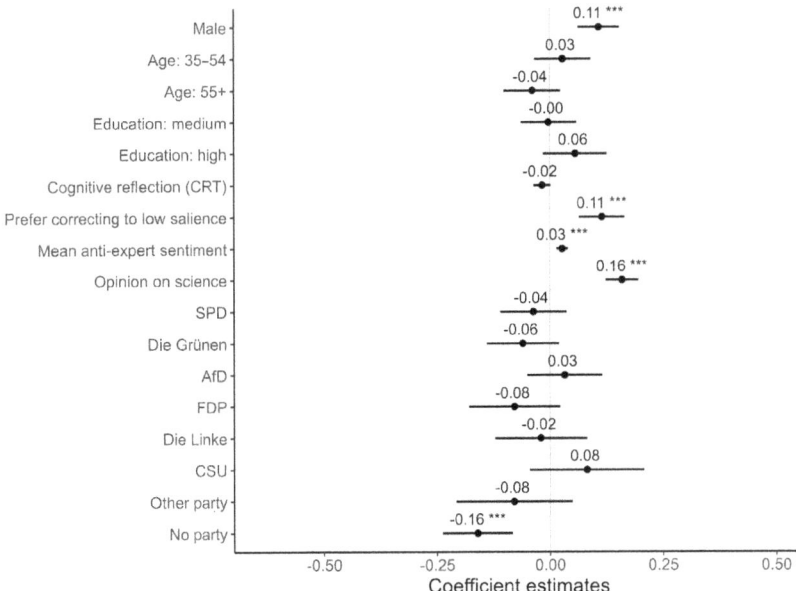

Figure 18 Determinants of subjective ability to correct false social media content.

Note: Survey question: "In most situations, I am able to correct false information." Response categories include: disagree completely, disagree somewhat, agree somewhat, agree completely. OLS regression, $N = 3,757$. Dots: point estimates, lines: 95 percent confidence interval. SPD: Social Democrats, Die Grünen: Green Party, AfD: Alternative for Germany, FDP: Liberal Party, Die Linke: Left Party, CSU: Bavarian part of Conservative Party. Reference groups: age under 35, female, education: low, party: Conservative (CDU), respondent prefers low salience over corrections of false information. Opinion on science (negative, rather negative, rather positive, positive). CRT: higher values represent higher cognitive reflection test (CRT) capabilities. Anti-expert sentiment score: higher values indicate greater anti-expert sentiment (index consisting of three items; see online appendix). Statistical significance: *** $p < 0.001$

However, unlike willingness to write comments, age and CRT scores are now insignificant. While younger and less cognitively effortful respondents are more likely to actually write comments, they express no greater sense of ability than their older and more cognitively reflective counterparts.

It is worth exploring in greater depth the findings regarding education and cognitive reflection on one hand and anti-expert positions on the other. As Table 4 shows, most respondents are confident in their abilities. 70 percent of those in

Table 4 Education, anti-expert positions, cognitive reflection, and commenting on misinformation

	Subjective ability to correct false online content			Self-reported correction frequency		
	Low	High		Never, rarely	Often/most of the time	
	27.4	72.6	100.0	78.8	21.2	100.0
By education level						
Low	30.2	69.8	100.0	78.1	21.9	100.0
Medium	28.6	71.4	100.0	79.5	20.5	100.0
High	23.1	76.9	100.0	78.0	22.0	100.0
By anti-expert sentiment score						
Low	29.7	70.3	100.0	84.4	15.7	100.0
Medium	26.5	73.5	100.0	80.1	19.9	100.0
High	21.0	79.0	100.0	58.0	42.0	100.0
By cognitive reflection score						
Low (0)	28.2	71.8	100.0	75.1	24.9	100.0
Medium (1)	28.3	71.7	100.0	76.6	23.4	100.0
High (2)	26.1	73.9	100.0	80.9	19.2	100.0
Very high (3+4)	26.6	73.4	100.0	83.7	16.3	100.0

Note: Table shows percentages. Authors' data. Survey fielded in Germany in February 2023 with population quotas on gender, age, education, and region. Subjective ability to correct false online content: "In most situations, I am able to correct false information." Disagree completely, disagree somewhat = Low, agree somewhat, agree completely = High. Self-reported correction frequency: respondents were asked "What do you do when you see false information on social media?" For each of six behaviors, we asked about the frequency at which this occurs. Table above refers to "writing comments and saying what was false."

the low education group and the lower tercile of anti-expert views feel confident in their ability, and this rises to 77 and 79 percent in the high education and high anti-expert groups, respectively. Confidence is similarly high across levels of CRT as well. When considering actual self-reports of behavior though – whether they actually engage in corrective commenting – differences emerge. Only about 22 percent of the highly educated post comments often or most of the time, about the same as the average respondent, and among those scoring highest in CRT, only about 16 percent write corrective corrections often or most of the time. Meanwhile we see significant variation across the anti-expert measure. A considerable number – 42 percent – of those most opposed to experts say they post corrections often or most of the time, compared to just about 16 percent of those with the most positive views toward experts.

This sizable imbalance suggests anti-expert positions are overrepresented in comments. This may also suggest that the content produced by the most prolific commenters is less accurate on average, particularly if they consistently contradict expert consensus (Light et al., 2022), though we cannot assess this. This result should be understood in the context of what others have found about those with anti-expert views instead: They are not only less knowledgeable, but also more vocal, and more likely to spread dubious news online (Light et al., 2022; Motta et al., 2018; Lyons et al., 2021), which may lead to misperceptions of the prevalence of their extreme views over time (McKeever et al., 2016).

One takeaway from these analyses may be to target those who are likely to be better equipped to correct misinformation but who otherwise refrain from doing so. For instance, respondents high in cognitive reflection reported engaging in corrections less often. This makes sense because cognitive reflection is a measure designed to gauge one's tendency to override an incorrect intuition, or "gut" response – a tendency quite opposed to confidently spreading a wrong message unchecked. But as others have consistently found, cognitive reflection is associated with better discernment between true and false news (Pennycook & Rand, 2019b, 2020) and sharing better quality news in real-world social media settings (Mosleh et al., 2021). Improving confidence or otherwise incentivizing the cognitively reflective to engage in corrective action is one potential route to improving the quality of online discussions.

5.5 Conclusion

In sum, we find that many social media users say they avoid engaging in corrective actions. Aside from interpersonal costs, one reason appears to be that they assign responsibility to platforms to police such content. They also believe that user comments can further muddy the waters of what's true and what's false. Still, they see corrections as valuable, and preferable to inaction even at the cost of increasing visibility to false content. When examining who is more likely to engage in corrective action, we find that those who have negative views of experts are more likely to feel that they can effectively post corrections, and self-report that they do so more often than those who view experts favorably. Taken together with our finding about the effects of miscorrections, this paints a troubling picture of the potential dynamics of online comments.

6 Implications and Outlook

In this concluding section, we offer some final arguments about the value of social corrections and potential applications going forward. We found that corrections can help users spot false information, but we have also shown that miscorrections can mislead social media users. These results were replicated several times across different contexts. Thus, the comparative nature of our data underscores the regularity of the observed effects across countries and topics, strengthening our confidence in these findings.

It is reasonable to ask why we might still see value in user-generated correction when we have demonstrated that miscorrections can be influential and commenters with anti-expert views may be among the most prolific commenters. In our view, there are a few pieces of good news that help mitigate these potential downsides. To begin, prior works suggest that crowd-sourced corrections could be effective: As Pennycook and Rand (2019a) show, in aggregate, higher-credibility news outlets are recognized as such, and aggregate ratings are on par with those of professional fact-checkers. Those higher in cognitive reflection were especially good at recognizing source quality; these individuals should especially be incentivized to engage in social corrections. A study employing natural language processing (NLP) tools also shows that comments on false news in the wild are more likely to express disbelief than comments on true news (Metzger et al., 2021). Mechanisms that filter public corrective comments – surfaced when a threshold of consensus is reached, as in the Community Notes feature of X (formerly Twitter) – could be a useful way to harness social corrections. There are, however, complications when these mechanisms are used as replacements for professional fact-checking rather than as a complementary system. With these considerations in mind, we conclude our Element with a practical outlook: We review best practices informed by our findings and discuss the potential future of social corrections in light of generative AI.

6.1 Writing Effective Corrections

Identifying false news on social media can be challenging (and can be more challenging for some). The false news that we used in our fieldwork was considered true by at least one out of five respondents. When false claims align with one's political predispositions, then respondents in our studies were more likely to perceive these headlines as accurate. Similarly (and consistent with prior research), individuals with less developed cognitive reflection skills are less able to identify false news, as are those with far-right or anti-expert positions. Based on the fieldwork from three countries, however, we find that social corrections can help people to identify false news in spite of these individual differences. Our results allow us to identify a set of best practices for how users could approach corrections.

It is first worth reflecting on the audience for corrections: The target audience for a correction is other users who see the original post. Thus, corrective comments can be useful even if they do not convince the original poster that their post contains false news. Posts can be seen by thousands of people – helping this audience navigate what is true and false in their social media feed is perhaps the most useful aspect of social corrections. This use case is different from debating with a potential stranger about the accuracy of content they have shared online. The person sharing inaccurate content might have truly overlooked that the information they shared is inaccurate, or they might have shared it in spite of the fact that they know it is flawed (Munyaka et al., 2022; Littrell et al., 2023). In these situations, corrections might positively affect the account sharing misinformation. However, it might also be the case that challenging the accuracy of a claim has no effect on the person who posted or shared it in the first instance. Being unable to change the original poster's mind does not mean that corrective comments are in vain; rather, as our research and the results from others have shown, comments can help other people to identify false information. That is, social corrections are not primarily thought to change worldviews or established false beliefs of the posters, but instead are mainly to help people decide more carefully on the accuracy of information that shows up in their feed. This more nuanced view of the audience for corrections allows us to appropriately think about how to maximize the effectiveness of corrections.

We wanted to explore different ways that corrections could be made more powerful or send a stronger signal. One specific component we examined was whether corrective posts that linked to a fact-check would have a stronger effect. We do not find comments with a fact checking link to be more effective than simple corrections. This finding somewhat lowers the bar of effort for those who want to write corrective comments. Users considering writing a corrective comment do not need to search for a fact-check to include in their comment to bolster the authority and veracity of their position. Yet, we do not take the fact that inclusion of a fact-checking link has minimal effect on increasing the effectiveness of a correction to mean that fact-checking as a journalistic enterprise is pointless. Providing such links improves the quality of the information in the comment for those who might encounter it, as they can more easily check the corrective claim. (Our experimental design does not provide users with the opportunity to click through to links when they are included in comments.) Providing a link is likely associated with increased deliberation exerted by the commenter and the odds that they themselves have avoided posting a miscorrection. As human beings, we are all subject to the same biases: Those who comment are also more likely to reject information that challenges their worldview, and they are more likely to post a correction in line with their worldview but maybe not in line with the facts. Consulting a fact-checking website can serve as an important buffer against this bias. The same strategies that help people identify false news in the first place (Wineburg & McGrew, 2017; Guess et al., 2020) should help people to make sure that they are not contributing to spreading false news.

Our results also reveal that corrections with a higher number of likes are not more effective in reducing perceived accuracy than comments with a few likes. When we showed respondents more corrective comments rather than just one, we did not observe stronger effects, either. However, this does not imply that likes (or additional comments) are irrelevant. We designed our treatments so that respondents would see the corrective comments, for example, by showing them right below a post. While the number of likes did not matter in how people responded to our treatments, the number of likes will play a factor in whether a comment is displayed in real world social media feeds. When corrective comments get more likes, the odds that this comment will be a featured one that appears automatically below a post is increased. In a competitive landscape in the attention economy, more likes may change the probability that a post is shown to users, making those comments more effective in real world settings, even if the number of likes has no direct effect on the persuasiveness of the comment (conditional on exposure). Liking a corrective comment by another user can help to ensure that it is visible among the top comments of a post. (Indeed, this is another way that fact-checking links may be helpful – they look more persuasive and garner additional likes as a result, increasing the chances the comment is easily seen in someone's feed.)

In a similar vein, additional comments could make corrective comments salient. As people reply to a comment to show their agreement, this may upweight the original comment. Our experimental manipulations suggest that once corrective comments are salient, additional likes or comments do not increase the corrective signal strength. But, additional reactions or comments might change the likelihood that the corrective comment is shown to other users (even if the corrective strength stays constant). These processes can be dynamic: A corrective comment that is salient in one moment may not be the top comment a few minutes, hours, or days later. Organic responses to content – especially if something goes even semi-viral – could quickly change the visibility of corrective comments.

One concern that people might have about posting corrections is that doing so contributes to the spread of misinformation as this engagement feeds into the social media algorithm thereby pushing the false content into more people's feeds. While we cannot answer questions about the algorithmic mechanics of how engagement changes the likelihood of "treating" new people with false content in their feeds, we can address questions about how people feel about this potential trade-off when engaging in corrective activity. Based on the results from Section 5, three out of four people prefer inaccurate content to be corrected, even if it makes misinformation more salient. Thus, more people are likely to appreciate corrective comments than to see it negatively. If the visibility of a comment – or any engagement with a false news post – is an obstacle for someone who is eager to get involved, they could also flag a post to the social media platform directly. Most platforms offer this option to flag content, though it requires more effort on some platforms than others (and default options for labelling problematic content do not always include an option for "false"). Using this approach also comes with the advantage of not contributing to the salience of a piece of false news. The downside is, however, that the consequence of this reporting is not clear either. While platforms claim to be interested in combating false information, traffic is essential for their business model. Social media platform policies do not necessarily prohibit false content, and there are often issue-by-issue policies. Moreover, the threshold and time frame for deletions as a result of content flagging is unknown. Finally, content-flagging by users is not without peril as users could flag content erroneously, and how platforms deal with these is not clear cut.

Commenting is a simple behavior, and one that shows promise as a strategy to address false claims in online social media spaces. If people were to inculcate the habit of writing social corrections as part of good social media hygiene, it would have the potential to improve online discourse. Just as there is evidence that casting a ballot in one election can increase the odds one turns out to the polls in the next election (e.g., Gerber et al., 2003), getting the bulk of social media users who never leave corrective comments to try it on an (initially) limited basis could result in significant aggregate improvements to the information environment long term.

6.2 Outlook: AI and Social Correction

Artificial intelligence (AI) is powerful and can be abused to disinform others on social media. However, these technologies may also enhance our corrective capacities. In this final section, we explore these issues as a future frontier for social corrections.

Artificial intelligence – especially generative AI like large language models (LLMs) is receiving considerable research and public interest (Vicari & Komendatova, 2023). However, there is also potential for this technology to be abused to create swathes of misinformation. For instance, when asked the right questions, language-learning models like ChatGPT are able to mass-produce false content. It is even possible for such misinformation to spread accidentally. The responses by ChatGPT are not researched, and when asked for sources the tool may freely invent them and possibly fool the reader (De Angelis et al., 2023; Haupt & Marks, 2023). Thus, individuals who do not know this or who misuse the AI can contribute to the spread of misinformation.

Furthermore, deepfakes or fake images pose an issue concerning misinformation. The former are videos of people that have been modified by machine-learning tools (Paris & Donovan, 2019). A famous example of a fake image that received a lot of media attention would be the picture of Pope Francis in a white puffer jacket (Huang, 2023). Such false material can be particularly problematic since it is often difficult to recognize as AI-generated (Partadiredja et al., 2020). To combat this problem, social media companies like Meta have implemented AI tools themselves to analyze images and point out potentially fake ones to professional fact-checkers (Woodford, 2018). Nevertheless, they are unlikely to catch all AI-generated content. As Groh et al. (2022) find, artificial intelligence tools are not yet able to correctly identify all deepfakes they are presented with. Hence, deepfakes and other fake AI images may continue to be used to promote false news.

Relatedly, large numbers of bots on social media platforms may help spread misinformation. They often serve malicious purposes, like trying to sway public opinion through the dissemination of false information (Lazer et al., 2018; Bastos & Mercea, 2019). Although social bots have existed since at least 2008, their popularity has steadily increased due to their cost-effectiveness. According to a 2018 study by the Pew Research Centre, about 66 percent of all content on Twitter at that time stemmed from bots (Wojcik et al., 2018). Some bots are even equipped with AI technology, making them more able to respond to different content like a human would (Hajli et al., 2022), which may make distinguishing between real and fake accounts even more challenging.

Even though the development of AI has caused several difficulties concerning misinformation, it may also help to address them. Some literature suggests that AI could be used to detect bots, deepfakes, and other misleading content. Shabani and Sohkn (2018), for example, advocate for the use of an AI that recognizes its weaknesses when detecting misinformation and asks for human input when necessary. However, there may also be other approaches, as suggested by Sager et al. (2021), for instance. In an experiment they used bots with natural language processing to post corrective comments on a Reddit forum on dermatology, with test accuracies from 95 to 100 percent. According to another idea by Lu et al. (2022), an AI may come up with credibility ratings for articles. This approach has been found to influence readers and, hence, may be another viable option to combat false news content – given that the AI is sufficiently accurate.

However, these solutions are likely not as straightforward as they appear. For instance, most of these approaches require a certain level of trust in AI, which may not always be present. Although several factors can determine such attitudes (Molina & Sundar, 2022), Wojcieszak et al. (2021) find that individuals generally have more trust in content moderation by humans than artificial intelligence. Moreover, an AI tool may be biased due to the data it was given to train it (Demartini, Mizzaro & Spina, 2020). As Groh et al. (2022) explain, this is one of the reasons why humans are more suited to moderate content. Lastly, the delicacy of freedom of speech may require a human to be responsible for determining what false or misleading content can be blocked. While some have argued for a more stringent filtering of content with AI before it is posted, this raises additional concerns about censorship (Dias Oliva, 2020; Llansó, 2020). Hence, many measures using AI are problematic due to the possible bias of AI and the implications on freedom of speech.

AI is already being employed by companies like Meta to detect misinformation and flag it for fact-checkers. Such uses may aid the fight against misinformation as it is a more time-efficient way to look for misleading content (Woodford, 2018; Gillespie, 2020). However, extending the use of AI to delete content has many negative implications on matters like freedom of speech and cannot be recommended (Dias Oliva, 2020; Gillespie, 2020; Llansó, 2020). Therefore, AI may only be a tool to tackle misinformation when it is used with care and to aid fact-checkers rather than to take over their jobs.

We show that user-driven approaches to debunking misinformation can be effective, but we also reveal important limitations of such efforts. Our research was conducted in an environment where fact-checking organizations played a significant role, even though corrections that included links to the fact-checkers' websites did not significantly increase their effectiveness. Nevertheless, the availability of professional fact-checkers' expertise remains crucial for users to verify the accuracy of corrections, thereby reducing the risk of miscorrections. Fact-checking organizations provide specialized knowledge that users do not necessarily possess, and they make high-quality debunks readily accessible. In this way, professional fact-checkers are an integral component of effective user-driven corrections, rather than an alternative. User-driven systems face critical limitations, particularly when deployed as substitutes for professional fact-checking rather than as complementary tools. Community Note systems usually flag content based on user consensus, which is determined algorithmically. Without the input of fact-checking organizations, the burden of fact-checking content is shifted to unpaid users while the availability of reliable debunking resources is simultaneously decreased. This risks undermining the overall quality of information on social media platforms. Overall, community-based approaches are likely most effective when combined with the expertise of professional fact-checkers.

In sum, we have offered some final arguments about the value of social corrections and potential applications going forward. We stress that social correction *in aggregate* may outweigh the insidious side effects of miscorrections, particular if the best commenters are incentivized or if comments are filtered in some way. In addition to some practice advice for commenters, we have also highlighted the perils and promise that an AI-infused future holds for the act of social correction.

References

Abascal, M., Huang, T. J., and Tran, V. C. (2021). Intervening in anti-immigrant sentiments: The causal effects of factual information on attitudes toward immigration. *The ANNALS of the American Academy of Political and Social Science*, 697(1), pp.174–191.

Abeler, J., Nosenzo, D., and Raymond, C. (2019). Preferences for truth-telling. *Econmetrica*, 87(4), pp.1115–1153.

Abualsaud, M. and Smucker, M. D. (2019). Exposure and order effects of misinformation on health search decisions. In *Proceedings of the Workshop on Relevance of Online Information to Medical Enquiries*. https://mustafa-s.com/papers/SIGIR2019/ROME/rome.pdf.

Acerbi, A., Altay, S., and Mercier, H. (2022). Research note: Fighting misinformation or fighting for information? *Harvard Kennedy School Misinformation Review*. https://doi.org/10.37016/mr-2020-87.

Ali, A. and Qazi, I. A. (2022). Cognitive reflection is associated with greater truth discernment for COVID-19 headlines, less trust but greater use of formal information sources, and greater willingness to pay for masks among social media users in Pakistan. *Harvard Kennedy School Misinformation Review*. https://doi.org/10.37016/mr-2020-101.

American Press Institute (2017). "My" media versus "the" media: Trust in news depends on which news media you mean. https://americanpressinstitute.org/my-media-vs-the-media/.

Anspach, N. M. (2017). The new personal influence: How our Facebook friends influence the news we read. *Political Communication*, 34(4), pp.590–606.

Anspach, N. M. and Carlson, T. N. (2020). What to believe? Social media commentary and belief in misinformation. *Political Behavior*, 42(3), pp.697–718.

Arechar, A. A., Allen, J., Berinsky, A. J., et al. (2023). Understanding and combatting misinformation across 16 countries on six continents. *Nature Human Behaviour*, 7(9), pp.1502–1513.

Asch, S. E. (1951). Effects of group pressure on the modification and distortion of judgements. In H. Guetzknow (ed.), *Groups, Leadership and Men*. Pittsburgh, PA: Carnegie Press, pp.177–190.

Asch, S. E. (1956). Studies of independence and conformity: I. A minority of one against a unanimous majority. *Psychological Monographs: General and Applied*, 70, pp.1–70. https://doi.org/10.1037/h0093718.

Badrinathan, S. and Chauchard, S. (2023). "I don't think that's true, bro!": Social corrections of misinformation in India. *The International Journal of Press/Politics*, 29(2), pp.394–416. https://doi.org/10.1177/19401612231158770.

Bago, B. and Pennycook, G. (2020). Fake news, fast and slow: Deliberation reduces belief in false (but not true) news headlines. *Journal of Experimental Psychology: General*, 149(8), pp.1608–1613. https://doi.org/10.1037/xge0000729.

Bastos, M. T. and Mercea, D. (2019). The Brexit botnet and user-generated hyperpartisan news. *Social Science Computer Review*, 37, pp.38–54. https://doi.org/10.1177/0894439317734157.

Baum, J. and Abdel Rahman, R. (2021). Emotional news affects social judgments independent of perceived media credibility. *Social Cognitive and Affective Neuroscience*, 16, pp.280–291. https://doi.org/10.1093/scan/nsaa164.

Bayes, R. and Druckman, J. N. (2021). Motivated reasoning and climate change. *Current Opinion in Behavioural Sciences*, 42, pp.27–35.

Bode, L. (2016). Pruning the news feed: Unfriending and unfollowing political content on social media. *Research & Politics*, 3(3), pp.1–8. https://doi.org/10.1177/2053168016661873.

Bode, L. (2017). Using expert sources to correct health misinformation in social media. *Science Communication*, 39(5), pp.621–645. https://doi.org/10.1177/1075547017731776.

Bode, L. and Vraga, E. K. (2017). Studying politics across media. *Political Communication*, 35(2), pp.1–7.

Bode, L. and Vraga, E. K. (2018). See something, say something: Correction of global health misinformation on social media. *Health Communication*, 33(9), pp.1131–1140. https://doi.org/10.1080/10410236.2017.1331312.

Bode, L. and Vraga, E. (2021a). Value for correction: Documenting perceptions about peer correction of misinformation on social media in the context of COVID-19. *Journal of Quantitative Description: Digital Media*, 1, pp.1–22. https://doi.org/10.51685/jqd.2021.016.

Bode, L. & Vraga, E. K. (2021b). Correction experiences on social media during COVID-19. *Social Media + Society*, 7(2). https://doi.org/10.1177/20563051211008829.

Bond, R. M., Fariss, C. J., Jones, J. J., et al. (2012). A 61-million-person experiment in social influence and political mobilization. *Nature*, 489, pp.295–298. https://doi.org/10.1038/nature11421.

Boot, A. B., Dijkstra, K., and Zwaan, R. A. (2021). The processing and evaluation of news content on social media is influenced by peer-user commentary. *Humanities and Social Sciences Communications*, 8(1), 209. https://doi.org/10.1057/s41599-021-00889-5.

Brashier, N. M. and Marsh, E. J. (2020). Judging truth. *Annual Review of Psychology*, 71, pp.499–515. https://doi.org/10.1146/annurev-psych-010419-050807.

Bronstein, M. V., Pennycook, G., Bear, A., Rand, D. G., and Cannon, T. D. (2019). Belief in fake news is associated with delusionality, dogmatism, religious fundamentalism, and reduced analytic thinking. *Journal of Applied Research in Memory and Cognition*, 8, pp.108–117. https://doi.org/10.1016/j.jarmac.2018.09.005.

Brunel, F. and Nelson, M. (2003). Message order effects and gender differences in advertising persuasion. *Journal of Advertising Research*, 43, pp.330–341. https://doi.org/10.1017/S0021849903030320.

Bryanov, K. and Vziatysheva, V. (2021). Determinants of individuals' belief in fake news: A scoping review determinants of belief in fake news. *PLOS ONE*, 16(6), e0253717. https://doi.org/10.1371/journal.pone.0253717.

Buchanan, T. (2020). Why do people spread false information online? The effects of message and viewer characteristics on self-reported likelihood of sharing social media disinformation. *PLOS ONE*, 15(10), e0239666. https://doi.org/10.1371/journal.pone.0239666.

Cacciatore, M. A. (2021). Misinformation and public opinion of science and health: Approaches, findings, and future directions. *Proceedings of the National Academy of Sciences*, 118(15), e1912437117. https://doi.org/10.1073/pnas.1912437117.

Carey, J. M., Guess, A. M., Loewen, P. J., et al. (2022). The ephemeral effects of fact-checks on COVID-19 misperceptions in the United States, Great Britain and Canada. *Nature Human Behaviour*, 6(2), pp.236–243.

Carter, J. S. and Alford, C. (2023). Adoxastic publics: Facebook and the loss of civic strangeness. *Quarterly Journal of Speech*, 109, pp.176–198. https://doi.org/10.1080/00335630.2022.2139856.

Castellini, G., Savarese, M., and Graffigna, G. (2021). Online fake news about food: Self-evaluation, social influence, and the stages of change moderation. *International Journal of Environmental Research and Public Health*, 18(6), p.2934. https://doi.org/10.3390/ijerph18062934.

Chadwick, A. and Vaccari, C. (2019). News sharing on UK social media: Misinformation, disinformation, and correction. Loughborough University. Report. https://hdl.handle.net/2134/37720.

Chadwick, A., Vaccari, C., and Hall, N. A. (2023). What explains the spread of misinformation in online personal messaging networks? Exploring the role of conflict avoidance. *Digital Journalism*, 12(5), pp.574–593.

Chen, X., Sin, S.-C. J., Theng, Y.-L., and Lee, C. S. (2015). Why students share misinformation on social media: Motivation, gender, and study-level differences. *The Journal of Academic Librarianship*, 41, pp.583–592. https://doi.org/10.1016/j.acalib.2015.07.003.

Cheng, Y. and Luo, Y. (2020). The presumed influence of digital misinformation: examining US public's support for governmental restrictions versus corrective action in the COVID-19 pandemic. *Online Information Review*, 45(4), pp.834–852.

Chinn, S. and Hasell, A. (2023). Support for "doing your own research" is associated with COVID-19 misperceptions and scientific mistrust. *Harvard Kennedy School Misinformation Review*, 4(3), pp.1–15. https://doi.org/10.37016/mr-2020-117.

Chua, A. Y. K., Tee, C.-Y., Pang, A., and Lim, E.-P. (2017). The retransmission of rumor and rumor correction messages on Twitter. *American Behavioral Scientist*, 61, pp.707–723. https://doi.org/10.1177/0002764217717561.

Cialdini, R. and Goldstein, N. (2004). Social influence: Compliance and conformity. *Annual Review of Psychology*, 55, pp.591–621. https://doi.org/10.1146/annurev.psych.55.090902.142015.

Ciampaglia, G. L., Nematzadeh, A., Menczer, F., and Flammini, A. (2018). How algorithmic popularity bias hinders or promotes quality. *Scientific Reports*, 8(1), 15951. https://doi.org/10.1038/s41598-018-34203-2.

Clayton, K., Blair, S., Busam, J. A., et al. (2020). Real solutions for fake news? Measuring the effectiveness of general warnings and fact-check tags in reducing belief in false stories on social media. *Political Behavior*, 42, pp.1073–1095.

Clayton, K., Davis, J., Hinckley, K., and Horiuchi, Y. (2019). Partisan motivated reasoning and misinformation in the media: Is news from ideologically uncongenial sources more suspicious? *Japanese Journal of Political Science*, 20, pp.129–142. https://doi.org/10.1017/S1468109919000082.

Clifford, S. and Rainey, C. (2025). The limits (and strengths) of single-topic experiments. *Political Analysis*, 33(2), pp.164–170.

Colliander, J. (2019). "This is fake news": Investigating the role of conformity to other users' views when commenting on and spreading disinformation in social media. *Computers in Human Behavior*, 97, pp.202–215. https://doi.org/10.1016/j.chb.2019.03.032.

Coppock, A. (2023). *Persuasion in Parallel: How Information Changes Minds about Politics*. Chicago, IL: University of Chicago Press.

Dai, Y., Yu, W., and Shen, F. (2021). The effects of message order and debiasing information in misinformation correction. *International Journal of Communication*, 15, pp.1039–1059.

De Angelis, L., Baglivo, F., Arzilli, et al. (2023). ChatGPT and the rise of large language models: The new AI-driven infodemic threat in public health.

Frontiers in Public Health, 11, pp.1–8. https://doi.org/10.3389/fpubh.2023.1166120.

Del Vicario, M., Bessi, A., Zollo, F., et al. (2016). The spreading of misinformation online. *Proceedings of the National Academy of Sciences*, 113(3), pp.554–559.

Demartini, G., Mizzaro, S., and Spina, D. (2020). Human-in-the-loop artificial intelligence for fighting online misinformation: Challenges and opportunities. *Bulletin of the IEEE Computer Society Technical Committee on Data Engineering*, 43 (3), pp.65–74.

Dias Oliva, T. (2020). Content moderation technologies: Applying human rights standards to protect freedom of expression. *Human Rights Law Review*, 20, pp.607–640. https://doi.org/10.1093/hrlr/ngaa032.

Dias, N., Pennycook, G., and Rand, D. G. (2020). Emphasizing publishers does not effectively reduce susceptibility to misinformation on social media. *Harvard Kennedy School Misinformation Review*, 1(1), pp.1–12. https://doi.org/10.37016/mr-2020-001.

Dor, D. (2003). On newspaper headlines as relevance optimizers. *Journal of Pragmatics*, 35(5), pp.695–721. https://doi.org/10.1016/S0378-2166(02)00134-0.

Druckman, J. N. (2022). A framework for the study of persuasion. *Annual Review of Political Science*, 25, pp.65–88.

Ecker, U. K. H., Lewandowsky, S., Cheung, C. S. C., and Maybery, M. T. (2015). He did it! She did it! No, she did not! Multiple causal explanations and the continued influence of misinformation. *Journal of Memory and Language*, 85, pp.101–115. https://doi.org/10.1016/j.jml.2015.09.002.

Elga, A. (2007). Reflection and disagreement. *Noûs*, 41, pp.478–502. https://doi.org/10.1111/j.1468-0068.2007.00656.x.

Epstein, Z., Berinsky, A. J., Cole, R., Gully, A., Pennycook, G., and Rand, D. G. (2021). Developing an accuracy-prompt toolkit to reduce COVID-19 misinformation online. *Harvard Kennedy School Misinformation Review*, 2(3), pp.1–12, https://doi.org/10.37016/mr-2020-71.

Epstein, Z., Sirlin, N., Arechar, A., Pennycook, G., and Rand, D. (2023). The social media context interferes with truth discernment. *Science Advances*, 9(9), eabo6169. https://doi.org/10.1126/sciadv.abo6169.

Flynn, D. J., Nyhan, B., and Reifler, J. (2017). The nature and origins of misperceptions: Understanding false and unsupported beliefs about politics. *Advances in Political Psychology*, 38(S1), pp.127–150. https://doi.org/10.1111/pops.12394.

Friggeri, A., Adamic, L., Eckles, D., and Cheng, J. (2014). Rumor cascades. *ICWSM*, 8, pp.101–110. https://doi.org/10.1609/icwsm.v8i1.14559.

Gabielkov, M., Ramachandran, A., Chaintreau, A., and Legout, A. (2016). Social clicks: What and who gets read on Twitter? *SIGMETRICS Performance Evaluation Review*, 44(1), pp.179–192. https://doi.org/10.1145/2964791.2901462.

Garrett, R. K. (2011). Troubling consequences of online political rumoring. *Human Communication Research*, 37(2), pp.255–274. https://doi.org/10.1111/j.1468-2958.2010.01401.x.

Garrett, R. K., Weeks, B. E., and Neo, R. L. (2016). Driving a wedge between evidence and beliefs: How online ideological news exposure promotes political misperceptions. *Journal of Computer-Mediated Communication*, 21(5), pp.331–348.

Garz, M. and Szucs, F. (2023). Algorithmic selection and supply of political news on Facebook. *Information Economics and Policy*, 62, 101020. https://doi.org/10.1016/j.infoecopol.2023.101020.

Gawronski, B. (2021). Partisan bias in the identification of fake news. *Trends in Cognitive Sciences*, 25(9), pp.723–724. https://doi.org/10.1016/j.tics.2021.05.001.

Gelman, A. and Stern, H. (2006). The difference between "significant" and "not significant" is not itself statistically significant. *The American Statistician*, 60(4), pp.328–331. https://doi.org/10.1198/000313006X152649.

Gerber, A. S., Green, D. P., and Shachar, R. (2003). Voting may be habit-forming: Evidence from a randomized field experiment. *American Journal of Political Science*, 47(3), pp.540–550.

Gillespie, T. (2020). Content moderation, AI, and the question of scale. *Big Data & Society*, 7, 2053951720943234. https://doi.org/10.1177/2053951720943234.

Gimpel, H., Heger, S., Olenberger, C., and Utz, L. (2021). The effectiveness of social norms in fighting fake news on social media. *Journal of Management Information Systems*, 38(1), pp.196–221. https://doi.org/10.1080/07421222.2021.1870389.

Goel, V., Raj, S., and Ravichandran, P. (2018). In India, fake news on Whatsapp fuels mob violence: Officials blame rumormongers as death toll mounts. *The New York Times*. https://www.nytimes.com/interactive/2018/07/18/technology/whatsapp-india-killings.html.

Granovetter, M. S. (1973). The strength of weak ties. *American Journal of Sociology*, 78(6), pp.1360–1380. https://doi.org/10.1086/225469.

Groh, M., Epstein, Z., Firestone, C., and Picard, R. (2022). Deepfake detection by human crowds, machines, and machine-informed crowds. *Proceedings of the National Academy of Sciences*, 119(1), e2110013119. https://doi.org/10.1073/pnas.2110013119.

Guess, A., Aslett, K., Tucker, J., Bonneau, R., and Nagler, J. (2021). Cracking open the news feed: Exploring what U.S. Facebook users see and share with large-scale platform data. *Journal of Quantitative Description: Digital Media*, 1, pp.1–48. https://doi.org/10.51685/jqd.2021.006.

Guess, A. M., Lerner, M., Lyons, B. A., et al. (2020). A digital media literacy intervention increases discernment between mainstream and false news in the United States and India. *Proceedings of the National Academy of Sciences*, 117(27), pp.15536–15545. https://doi.org/10.1073/pnas.1920498117.

Guess, A. M. and Lyons, B. A. (2020). Misinformation, disinformation, and online propaganda. In N. Persily and J. A. Tucker, *Social Media and Democracy: The State of the Field, Prospects for Reform*. Cambridge, UK: Cambridge University Press, pp.10–33.

Guess, A. M., Lyons, B. A., Nyhan, B., and Reifler, J. (2018). Avoiding the echo chamber about echo chambers. *Knight Foundation*, 2(1), pp.1–25.

Guess, A. M., Nagler, J., and Tucker, J. (2019). Less than you think: Prevalence and predictors of fake news dissemination on Facebook. *Science Advances*, 5(1), eaau4586.

Gurgun, S., Cemiloglu, D., Arden-Close, E., Phalp, K., Nakov, P., and Ali, R. (2023). Challenging misinformation on social media: Users' perceptions and misperceptions and their impact on the willingness to challenge. *SSRN*, 4440292. https://dx.doi.org/10.2139/ssrn.4440292.

Haigh, M. (2016). Has the standard cognitive reflection test become a victim of its own success? *Advances in Cognitive Psychology*, 12(3), pp.145–149. https://doi.org/10.5709/acp-0193-5.

Hajli, N., Saeed, U., Tajvidi, M., and Shirazi, F. (2022). Social bots and the spread of disinformation in social media: The challenges of artificial intelligence. *British Journal of Management*, 33(3), pp.1238–1253. https://doi.org/10.1111/1467-8551.12554.

Hameleers, M., Brosius, A., and de Vreese, C. (2022). Whom to trust? Media exposure patterns of citizens with perceptions of misinformation and disinformation related to the news media. *European Journal of Communication*, 37(3), pp.237–268. https://doi.org/10.1177/02673231211072667.

Han, H., Blackburn, A. M., Jeftić, A., et al. (2022). Validity testing of the conspiratorial thinking and anti-expert sentiment scales during the COVID-19 pandemic across 24 languages from a large-scale global dataset. *Epidemiology and Infection*, 150, e167. https://doi.org/10.1017/S0950268822001443.

Haugtvedt, C. P. and Wegener, D. T. (1994). Message order effects in persuasion: An attitude strength perspective. *Journal of Consumer Research*, 21(1), pp.205–218.

Haupt, C. E., Marks, M. (2023). AI-generated medical advice—GPT and beyond. *JAMA*, 329(16), pp.1349–1350. https://doi.org/10.1001/jama.2023.5321.

Huang, K. (2023). Why Pope Francis is the star of A.I.-generated photos. *The New York Times*. https://www.nytimes.com/2023/04/08/technology/ai-photos-pope-francis.html.

Huang, Y., Wang, W. (2022). When a story contradicts: Correcting health misinformation on social media through different message formats and mechanisms. *Information, Communication & Society*, 25(8), pp.1192–1209. https://doi.org/10.1080/1369118X.2020.1851390.

Humprecht, E., Esser, F., Aelst, P.V., Staender, A., and Morosoli, S. (2023). The sharing of disinformation in cross-national comparison: Analyzing patterns of resilience. *Information, Communication & Society*, 26(7), pp.1342–1362.

Hunt, K., Wang, B., and Zhuang, J. (2020). Misinformation debunking and cross-platform information sharing through Twitter during Hurricanes Harvey and Irma: A case study on shelters and ID checks. *Natural Hazards*, 103, pp.861–883. https://doi.org/10.1007/s11069-020-04016-6.

Jackson, S. J. and Foucault Welles, B., (2015). Hijacking #MYNYPD: Social media dissent and networked counterpublics. *Journal of Communication*, 65(6), pp.932–952. https://doi.org/10.1111/jcom.12185.

Jakesch, M., Koren, M., Evtushenko, A., and Naaman, M. (2018). The role of source, headline and expressive responding in political news evaluation. *SSRN*. https://doi.org/10.2139/ssrn.3306403.

Johnson, T. and Kromka, S. M. (2023). Psychological, communicative, and relationship characteristics that relate to social media users' willingness to denounce fake news. *Cyberpsychology, Behavior, and Social Networking*, 26(7), pp.563–571. https://doi.org/10.1089/cyber.2022.0204.

Kalogeropoulos, A., Negredo, S., Picone, I. and Nielsen, R.K. (2017). Who shares and comments on news?: A cross-national comparative analysis of online and social media participation. *Social Media + Society*, 3(4), p.2056305117735754.

Kaplan, D., (2021). Public intimacy in social media: The mass audience as a third party. *Media, Culture & Society*, 43, pp.595–612. https://doi.org/10.1177/0163443721991087.

Karras, T., Laine, S. and Aila, T. (2019). A style-based generator architecture for generative adversarial networks. In *Proceedings of the IEEE/CVF Conference on Computer Vision and Pattern Recognition*, pp.4401–4410. https://doi.org/10.1109/CVPR.2019.00453.

Kim, A. and Dennis, A. (2019). Says who? The effects of presentation format and source rating on fake news in social media. *MIS Quarterly*, 43(3), pp.1025–1039. https://doi.org/10.25300/MISQ/2019/15188.

Kim, A., Moravec, P., and Dennis, A. (2019). Combating fake news on social media with source ratings: The effects of user and expert reputation ratings. *Journal of Management Information Systems*, 36(3), pp.931–968. https://doi.org/10.1080/07421222.2019.1628921.

Kim, H., Han, J. Y., and Seo, Y. (2020). Effects of Facebook comments on attitude toward vaccines: The roles of perceived distributions of public opinion and perceived vaccine efficacy. *Journal of Health Communication*, 25(2), pp.159–169. https://doi.org/10.1080/10810730.2020.1723039.

Kim, J. W., Guess, A., Nyhan, B., and Reifler, J. (2021). The distorting prism of social media: How self-selection and exposure to incivility fuel online comment toxicity. *Journal of Communication*, 71(6), pp.922–946.

King, K.K., Wang, B., Escobari, D., and Oraby, T. (2021). Dynamic effects of falsehoods and corrections on social media: A theoretical modeling and empirical evidence. *Journal of Management Information Systems*, 38(4), pp.989–1010. https://doi.org/10.1080/07421222.2021.1990611.

Kozyreva, A., Herzog, S. M., Lewandowsky, S., et al. (2023). Resolving content moderation dilemmas between free speech and harmful misinformation. *Proceedings of the National Academy of Sciences*, 120, p.e2210666120. https://doi.org/10.1073/pnas.2210666120.

Krech, D., Crutchfield, R. S., and Ballachey, E. L. (1962). *Individual in Society: A Textbook of Social Psychology*. New York, NY: McGraw-Hill.

Lazer, D. M. J., Baum, M. A., Benkler, Y., et al. (2018). The science of fake news. *Science*, 359(6380), pp.1094–1096. https://doi.org/10.1126/science.aao2998.

Leeder, C. (2019). How college students evaluate and share "fake news" stories. *Library & Information Science Research*, 41(3), p.100967. https://doi.org/10.1016/j.lisr.2019.100967.

Levy, N. (2023). What does the CRT measure? Poor performance may arise from rational processes. *Philosophical Psychology*, 36(1), pp.58–84. https://doi.org/10.1080/09515089.2022.2038123.

Lewandowsky, S., Cook, J., Ecker, U. K., and Newman, E. J. (2020). *Under the Hood of The Debunking Handbook 2020: A Consensus-Based Handbook of Recommendations for Correcting or Preventing Misinformation*. Center for Climate Change Communication. https://skepticalscience.com/docs/DebunkingHandbook2020-UnderTheHood.pdf.

Light, N., Fernbach, P. M., Rabb, N., Geana, M. V., and Sloman, S. A. (2022). Knowledge overconfidence is associated with anti-consensus views on controversial scientific issues. *Science Advances*, 8(29), p.eabo0038.

Little, A. T. (2021). Directional motives and different priors are observationally equivalent. University of California-Berkeley (unpublished manuscript), pp.1–31.

Littrell, S., Klofstad, C., Diekman, A., et al. (2023). Who knowingly shares false political information online? *Harvard Kennedy School Misinformation Review*, 4(4). https://doi.org/10.37016/mr-2020-121.

Llansó, E. J. (2020). No amount of "AI" in content moderation will solve filtering's prior-restraint problem. *Big Data & Society*, 7(1), p.2053951720920686. https://doi.org/10.1177/2053951720920686.

Lowe-Calverley, E. and Grieve, R. (2018). Thumbs up: A thematic analysis of image-based posting and liking behaviour on social media. *Telematics and Informatics*, 35(7), pp.1900–1913.

Lu, Z., Li, P., Wang, W., and Yin, M. (2022). The effects of AI-based credibility indicators on the detection and spread of misinformation under social influence. *Proceedings of the ACM on Human-Computer Interaction*, 6, pp.1–27.

Luo, M., Hancock, J. T., and Markowitz, D. M. (2022). Credibility perceptions and detection accuracy of fake news headlines on social media: Effects of truth-bias and endorsement cues. *Communication Research*, 49(2), pp.171–195. https://doi.org/10.1177/0093650220921321.

Lupia, A. and McCubbins, M. D. (1998). *The Democratic Dilemma: Can Citizens Learn What They Need to Know?* Cambridge, UK: Cambridge University Press.

Lutzke, L., Drummond, C., Slovic, P., and Árvai, J. (2019). Priming critical thinking: Simple interventions limit the influence of fake news about climate change on Facebook. *Global Environmental Change*, 58, p.101964. https://doi.org/10.1016/j.gloenvcha.2019.101964.

Lyons, B. A. (2022a). Insidiously trivial: Meme format reduces perceived influence and intent to debate partisan claims. *Media and Communication*, 10(3), pp.196–205.

Lyons, B. A. (2022b). Why we should rethink the third-person effect: disentangling bias and earned confidence using behavioral data. *Journal of Communication*, 72(5), pp.565–577.

Lyons, B. A., Merola, V., and Reifler, J. (2020). Shifting medical guidelines: Compliance and spillover effects for revised antibiotic recommendations. *Social Science & Medicine*, 255, p.112943.

Lyons, B., Montgomery, J. M., Guess, A. M., et al. (2021). Overconfidence in news judgments is associated with false news susceptibility. *Proceedings of the National Academy of Sciences*, 118(23), p.e2019527118.

Lyons, B., Montgomery, J. M., and Reifler, J. (2024). Partisanship and older Americans' engagement with dubious political news. *Public Opinion Quarterly*, 88(3), pp.962–990. https://doi.org/10.31219/osf.io/etb89.

Margolin, D. B., Hannak, A., and Weber, I. (2018). Political fact-checking on Twitter: When do corrections have an effect? *Political Communication*, 35(2), pp.196–219. https://doi.org/10.1080/10584609.2017.1334018.

Margolin, D. B. and Liao, W. (2018). The emotional antecedents of solidarity in social media crowds. *New Media & Society*, 20(10), pp.3700–3719. https://doi.org/10.1177/1461444818758702.

Masullo, G. M. and Kim, J. (2021). Exploring "angry" and "like" reactions on uncivil Facebook comments that correct misinformation in the news. *Digital Journalism*, 9(8), pp.1103–1122. https://doi.org/10.1080/21670811.2020.1835512.

Masullo, G. M., Riedl, M. J., and Huang, Q. E. (2022). Engagement moderation: What journalists should say to improve online discussions. *Journalism Practice*, 16(4), pp.738–754. https://doi.org/10.1080/17512786.2020.1808858.

Masullo, G. M., Tenenboim, O., and Lu, S. (2023). "Toxic atmosphere effect": Uncivil online comments cue negative audience perceptions of news outlet credibility. *Journalism*, 24(1), pp.101–119. https://doi.org/10.1177/14648849211064001.

McKeever, B. W., McKeever, R., Holton, A. E., and Li, J. Y. (2016). Silent majority: Childhood vaccinations and antecedents to communicative action. *Mass Communication and Society*, 19(4), pp.476–498.

Mena, P., Barbe, D., Chan-Olmsted, S. (2020). Misinformation on Instagram: The impact of trusted endorsements on message credibility. *Social Media + Society*, 6(2), pp.1–9. https://doi.org/10.1177/2056305120935102.

Metzger, M. J., Flanagin, A. J., Mena, P., et al. (2021). From dark to light: The many shades of sharing misinformation online. *Media and Communication*, 9(1), pp.134–143.

Michael, R. B. and Breaux, B. O. (2021). The relationship between political affiliation and beliefs about sources of "fake news." *Cognitive Research: Principles and Implications*, 6. https://doi.org/10.1186/s41235-021-00278-1.

Modirrousta-Galian, A. and Higham, P. A. (2023). Gamified inoculation interventions do not improve discrimination between true and fake news: Reanalyzing existing research with receiver operating characteristic analysis. *Journal of Experimental Psychology: General*, 152(9), p.2411.

Molina, M. D. and Sundar, S. S. (2022). Does distrust in humans predict greater trust in AI? Role of individual differences in user responses to content moderation. *New Media & Society*, 26(6), pp.3638–3656. https://doi.org/10.1177/14614448221103534.

Moravec, P., Minas, R., and Dennis, A. (2018). Fake news on social media: People believe what they want to believe when it makes no sense at all. *SSRN*. https://doi.org/10.2139/ssrn.3269541.

Moretto, M., Ortellado, P., Kessler, G., et al. (2022). People are more engaged on Facebook as they get older, especially in politics: Evidence from users in

46 countries. *Journal of Quantitative Description: Digital Media*, 2, pp.1–20. https://doi.org/10.51685/jqd.2022.018.

Mosleh, M., Pennycook, G., Arechar, A. A., and Rand, D. G. (2021). Cognitive reflection correlates with behavior on Twitter. *Nature Communications*, 12, 921. https://doi.org/10.1038/s41467-020-20043-0.

Motta, M., Callaghan, T., and Sylvester, S. (2018). Knowing less but presuming more: Dunning-Kruger effects and the endorsement of anti-vaccine policy attitudes. *Social Science & Medicine*, 211, pp.274–281.

Munyaka, I., Hargittai, E., and Redmiles, E. (2022). The misinformation paradox: Older adults are cynical about news media, but engage with it anyway. *Journal of Online Trust and Safety*, 1(4), pp.1–15. https://doi.org/10.54501/jots.v1i4.62.

Naab, T. K., Heinbach, D., Ziegele, M., and Grasberger, M.-T. (2020). Comments and credibility: How critical user comments decrease perceived news article credibility. *Journalism Studies*, 21(4), pp.783–801. https://doi.org/10.1080/1461670X.2020.1724181.

Nadarevic, L., Reber, R., Helmecke, A. J., and Köse, D. (2020). Perceived truth of statements and simulated social media postings: an experimental investigation of source credibility, repeated exposure, and presentation format. *Cognitive Research: Principles and Implications*, 5, 56. https://doi.org/10.1186/s41235-020-00251-4.

Nadeau, R., Cloutier, E., and Guay, J. H. (1993). New evidence about the existence of a bandwagon effect in the opinion formation process. *International Political Science Review*, 14(2), pp.203–213.

Nan, X., Wang, Y., and Thier, K. (2022). Why do people believe health misinformation and who is at risk? A systematic review of individual differences in susceptibility to health misinformation. *Social Science & Medicine*, 314, 115398. https://doi.org/10.1016/j.socscimed.2022.115398.

Neubaum, G., Krämer, N. C. (2017). Monitoring the opinion of the crowd: Psychological mechanisms underlying public opinion perceptions on social media. *Media Psychology*, 20(3), pp.502–531. https://doi.org/10.1080/15213269.2016.1211539.

Newman, N., Fletcher, R., Eddy, K., Robertson, C. T., and Nielsen, R. K. (2023). *Digital News Report 2023*. Reuters Institute. https://reutersinstitute.politics.ox.ac.uk/sites/default/files/2023-06/Digital_News_Report_2023.pdf.

Nyhan, B. and Reifler, J. (2010). When corrections fail: The persistence of political misperceptions. *Political Behavior*, 32(2), pp.303–330.

Offer-Westort, M., Rosenzweig, L. R., and Athey, S. (2024). Battling the coronavirus 'infodemic' among social media users in Kenya and Nigeria. *Nature Human Behaviour* 8, pp.823–834. https://doi.org/10.1038/s41562-023-01810-7.

Osmundsen, M., Bor, A., Vahlstrup, P. B., Bechmann, A., and Petersen, M. B. (2021). Partisan polarization is the primary psychological motivation behind political fake news sharing on Twitter. *American Political Science Review*, 115(3), pp.999–1015. https://doi.org/10.1017/S0003055421000290.

Paasch-Colberg, S. and Strippel, C. (2022). "The boundaries are blurry...": How comment moderators in Germany see and respond to hate comments. *Journalism Studies*, 23(2), pp. 224–244. https://doi.org/10.1080/1461670X.2021.2017793.

Paris, B. and Donovan, J. (2019). Deepfakes and cheap fakes. Data & Society Research Institute. https://datasociety.net/wp-content/uploads/2019/09/DS_Deepfakes_Cheap_FakesFinal-1-1.pdf.

Partadiredja, R. A., Serrano, C. E., and Ljubenkov, D. (2020). AI or human: The socio-ethical implications of AI-generated media content. In *13th CMI Conference on Cybersecurity and Privacy (CMI) – Digital Transformation – Potentials and Challenges (51275)*, pp.1–6. https://doi.org/10.1109/CMI51275.2020.9322673.

Peacock, C. and Van Duyn, E. (2023). Monitoring and correcting: Why women read and men comment online. *Information, Communication & Society*, 26(6), pp.1106–1121. https://doi.org/10.1080/1369118X.2021.1993957.

Pehlivanoglu, D., Lighthall, N. R., Lin, T., et al. e(2022). Aging in an "infodemic": The role of analytical reasoning, affect, and news consumption frequency on news veracity detection. *Journal of Experimental Psychology: Applied*, 28(3), pp.468–485. https://doi.org/10.1037/xap0000426.

Pennycook, G., Binnendyk, J., Newton, C., and Rand, D. G. (2021a). A practical guide to doing behavioral research on fake news and misinformation. *Collabra: Psychology*, 7(1), p.25293. https://doi.org/10.1525/collabra.25293.

Pennycook, G., Epstein, Z., Mosleh, M., Arechar, A. A., Eckles, D. and Rand, D. G. (2021b). Shifting attention to accuracy can reduce misinformation online. *Nature*, 592(7855), pp.590–595.

Pennycook, G. and Rand, D. G. (2019a). Fighting misinformation on social media using crowdsourced judgments of news source quality. *Proceedings of the National Academy of Sciences*, 116, pp.2521–2526. https://doi.org/10.1073/pnas.1806781116.

Pennycook, G. and Rand, D. G. (2019b). Lazy, not biased: Susceptibility to partisan fake news is better explained by lack of reasoning than by motivated reasoning. *Cognition*, 188, pp.39–50.

Pennycook, G. and Rand, D. G. (2020). Who falls for fake news? The roles of bullshit receptivity, overclaiming, familiarity, and analytic thinking. *Journal of Personality*, 88(2), pp.185-200.

Pennycook, G. and Rand, D. G. (2021). The psychology of fake news. *Trends in Cognitive Sciences*, 25(5), pp.388–402. https://doi.org/10.1016/j.tics.2021.02.007.

Pereira, A., Harris, E., and Van Bavel, J. J. (2023). Identity concerns drive belief: The impact of partisan identity on the belief and dissemination of true and false news. *Group Processes & Intergroup Relations*, 26(1), pp.24–47. https://doi.org/10.1177/13684302211030004.

Petersen, M. B., Osmundsen, M., and Arceneaux, K. (2023). The "need for chaos" and motivations to share hostile political rumors. *American Political Science Review*, 117(4), pp.1486–1505.

Pretus, C., Servin-Barthet, C., Harris, E. A., Brady, W. J., Vilarroya, O., and Van Bavel, J. J. (2023). The role of political devotion in sharing partisan misinformation and resistance to fact-checking. *Journal of Experimental Psychology: General*, 152(11), pp.3116–3134. https://doi.org/10.1037/xge0001436.

Prike, T., Butler, L. H., and Ecker, U. K. H. (2024). Source-credibility information and social norms improve truth discernment and reduce engagement with misinformation online. *Scientific Reports* 14, 6900. https://doi.org/10.1038/s41598-024-57560-7.

Rahmanian, E. and Esfidani, M. R. (2023). It is probably fake but let us share it! Role of analytical thinking, overclaiming and social approval in sharing fake news. *Journal of Creative Communications*, 18(1), pp.7–25. https://doi.org/10.1177/09732586221116464.

Ratner, K. G., Dotsch, R., Wigboldus, D. H. J., van Knippenberg, A., and Amodio, D. M. (2014). Visualizing minimal ingroup and outgroup faces: Implications for impressions, attitudes, and behavior. *Journal of Personality and Social Psychology*, 106(6), pp.897–911. https://doi.org/10.1037/a0036498.

Reddi, M., Kuo, R., and Kreiss, D. (2023). Identity propaganda: Racial narratives and disinformation. *New Media & Society*, 25(8), pp.2201–2218.

Ribeiro, M. H., Jhaver, S., Reignier-Tayar, M., and West, R. (2024). Deplatforming norm-violating influencers on social media reduces overall online attention toward them. *arXiv preprint*. https://doi.org/10.48550/arXiv.2401.01253.

Robison, J. (2021). What's the value of partisan loyalty? Partisan ambivalence, motivated reasoning, and correct voting in US presidential elections. *Political Psychology*, 42(6), pp.977–993.

Roozenbeek, J., Van Der Linden, S., Goldberg, B., et al. (2022). Psychological inoculation improves resilience against misinformation on social media. *Science Advances*, 8(34), eabo6254.

Rossini, P., Mont'Alverne, C., and Kalogeropoulos, A. (2023). Explaining beliefs in electoral misinformation in the 2022 Brazilian election: The role of ideology, political trust, social media, and messaging apps. *Harvard Kennedy School Misinformation Review*, 4(3).

Sager, M. A., Kashyap, A. M., Tamminga, M., Ravoori, S., Callison-Burch, C., and Lipoff, J. B. (2021). Identifying and responding to health misinformation on Reddit dermatology forums with artificially intelligent bots using natural language processing: Design and evaluation study. *JMIR Dermatology*, 4(2), e20975. https://doi.org/10.2196/20975.

Saltz, E., Barari, S., Leibowicz, C., and Wardle, C. (2021). Misinformation interventions are common, divisive, and poorly understood. *Harvard Kennedy School Misinformation Review*, 2(5).

Sanderson, Z., Brown, M. A., Bonneau, R., Nagler, J., and Tucker, J. A. (2021). Twitter flagged Donald Trump's tweets with election misinformation: They continued to spread both on and off the platform. *Harvard Kennedy School Misinformation Review*, 2(4).

Schulz, J. F., Thiemann, P., and Thöni, C. (2018). Nudging generosity: Choice architecture and cognitive factors in charitable giving. *Journal of Behavioral and Experimental Economics*, 74, pp.139–145. https://doi.org/10.1016/j.socec.2018.04.001.

Schwarz, N., Newman, E., and Leach, W. (2016). Making the truth stick and the myths fade: Lessons from cognitive psychology. *Behavioural Science & Policy*, 2(1), pp.85–95. https://doi.org/10.1177/237946151600200110.

Shabani, S. and Sokhn, M. (2018). Hybrid machine-crowd approach for fake news detection. In *2018 IEEE 4th International Conference on Collaboration and Internet Computing (CIC)*, pp.299–306. https://doi.org/10.1109/CIC.2018.00048.

Shin, J., Jian, L., Driscoll, K., and Bar, F. (2017). Political rumoring on Twitter during the 2012 US presidential election: Rumor diffusion and correction. *New Media & Society*, 19(8), pp.1214–1235. https://doi.org/10.1177/1461444816634054.

Sindermann, C., Schmitt, H. S., Rozgonjuk, D., Elhai, J. D., and Montag, C. (2021). The evaluation of fake and true news: On the role of intelligence, personality, interpersonal trust, ideological attitudes, and news consumption. *Heliyon*, 7(3), e06503. https://doi.org/10.1016/j.heliyon.2021.e06503.

Spälti, A. K., Lyons, B., Stoeckel, F., et al. (2023). Partisanship and anti-elite worldviews as correlates of science and health beliefs in the multi-party system of Spain. *Public Understanding of Science*, 32(6), pp.761–780.

Spezzano, F., Shrestha, A., Fails, J. A., et al. (2021). That's fake news! Reliability of news when provided title, image, source bias & full article.

Proceedings of the ACM on Human-Computer Interaction, 5(CSCW1), pp.1–19. https://doi.org/10.1145/3449183.

Stanovich, K. E. (2021). Why humans are cognitive misers and what it means for the great rationality debate. *Routledge Handbook of Bounded Rationality*, London: Routledge, pp.196–206.

Steenbergen, M. R. and Jones, B. S. (2002). Modelling multilevel data structures. *American Journal of Political Science*, 46(1), pp.218–237. https://doi.org/10.2307/3088424.

Stöckli, S., Henry, S., and Bartsch, F. (2020). The darkside of online social networks: Measuring the negative effects of social influence in online social networks. https://boris.unibe.ch/id/eprint/153830.

Stöckli, S. and Hofer, D. (2020). Susceptibility to social influence predicts behavior on Facebook. *PLOS ONE*, 15, e0229337. https://doi.org/10.1371/journal.pone.0229337.

Stoeckel, F., Stöckli, S., Ceka, B., et al. (2024). Social corrections act as a double-edged sword by reducing the perceived accuracy of false and real news in the UK, Germany, and Italy. *Communications Psychology*, 2, 10. https://doi.org/10.1038/s44271-024-00057-w.

Suau, J., Masip, P., and Ruiz, C. (2019). Missing the big wave: Citizens' discourses against the participatory formats adopted by news media. *Journalism Practice*, 13(10), pp.1316–1332. https://doi.org/10.1080/17512786.2019.1591928.

Sun, P., Tsai, R., Finger, G., Chen, Y., and Yeh, D. (2008). What drives successful e-learning? An empirical investigation of the critical factors influencing learner satisfaction. *Computers and Education*, 50(4), pp.1183–1202.

Sundar, S. S. (2008). The MAIN model: A heuristic approach to understanding technology effects on credibility. In M. J. Metzger and A. J. Flanagin, *Digital Media, Youth, and Credibility*, Cambridge, MA: MIT Press, pp.73–100.

Swire-Thompson, B., DeGutis, J., and Lazer, D. (2020). Searching for the backfire effect: Measurement and design considerations. *Journal of Applied Research in Memory and Cognition*, 9(3), pp.286–299.

Swire, B., Berinsky, A. J., Lewandowsky, S., and Ecker, U. K. H. (2017). Processing political misinformation: comprehending the Trump phenomenon. *Royal Society Open Science*, 4, 160802. https://doi.org/10.1098/rsos.160802.

Swire, B., Ecker, U. K., and Lewandowsky, S. (2017). The role of familiarity in correcting inaccurate information. *Journal of Experimental Psychology: Learning, Memory, and Cognition*, 43(12), 1948.

Takayasu, M., Sato, K., Sano, Y., Yamada, K., Miura, W., and Takayasu, H. (2015). Rumor diffusion and convergence during the 3.11 earthquake:

A Twitter case study. *PLoS ONE*, 10. https://doi.org/10.1371/journal.pone.0121443.

Traberg, C. S. and van der Linden, S. (2022). Birds of a feather are persuaded together: Perceived source credibility mediates the effect of political bias on misinformation susceptibility. *Personality and Individual Differences*, 185, p.111269. https://doi.org/10.1016/j.paid.2021.111269.

Trepte, S. and Scherer, H. (2010). Opinion leaders: Do they know more than others about their area of interest? *Communications*, 35(2), pp.119–140.

Tucker, J. A., Guess, A., Barberá, P., et al. (2018). Social media, political polarization, and political disinformation: A review of the scientific literature. *SSRN*. https://dx.doi.org/10.2139/ssrn.3144139.

Tully, M., Bode, L., and Vraga, E. K. (2020). Mobilizing users: Does exposure to misinformation and its correction affect users' responses to a health misinformation post? *Social Media + Society*, 6(4), p.205630512097837. https://doi.org/10.1177/2056305120978377.

Tully, M., Madrid-Morales, D., Wasserman, H., Gondwe, G., and Ireri, K. (2022). Who is responsible for stopping the spread of misinformation? Examining audience perceptions of responsibilities and responses in six Sub-Saharan African countries. *Digital Journalism*, 10(5), pp.679–697.

Ulusoy, E., Carnahan, D., Bergan, D. E., et al. (2021). Flooding the zone: How exposure to implausible statements shapes subsequent belief judgments. *International Journal of Public Opinion Research*, 33(4), pp.856–872.

Uscinski, J. E., Enders, A. M., Seelig, M. I., et al. (2021). American politics in two dimensions: Partisan and ideological identities versus anti-establishment orientations. *American Journal of Political Science*, 65(4), pp.877–895.

Van der Linden, S., Malibach, E., Cook, J., Leiserowitz, A., and Lewandowsky, S. (2017). Inoculating against misinformation. *Science*, 358(6367), pp.1141–1142.

Van Duyn, E. and Collier, J. (2019). Priming and fake news: The effects of elite discourse on evaluations of news media. *Mass Communication and Society*, 22, pp.29–48. https://doi.org/10.1080/15205436.2018.1511807.

Vicari, R. and Komendatova, N. (2023). Systematic meta-analysis of research on AI tools to deal with misinformation on social media during natural and anthropogenic hazards and disasters. *Humanities and Social Sciences Communications*, 10, p.332. https://doi.org/10.1057/s41599-023-01838-0.

Vijaykumar, S., Rogerson, D. T., Jin, Y., et al. (2022). Dynamics of social corrections to peers sharing COVID-19 misinformation on WhatsApp in Brazil. *Journal of the American Medical Informatics Association*, 29(1), pp.33–42.

Vosoughi, S., Roy, D., and Aral, S. (2018). The spread of true and false news online. *Science*, 359, pp.1146–1151. https://doi.org/10.1126/science.aap9559.

Vraga, E. K. and Bode, L. (2017). Using expert sources to correct health misinformation in social media. *Science Communication*, 39(5), pp.621–645. https://doi.org/10.1177/1075547017731776.

Vraga, E. K. and Bode, L. (2018). I do not believe you: How providing a source corrects health misperceptions across social media platforms. *Information, Communication & Society*, 21(10), pp.1337–1353. https://doi.org/10.1080/1369118X.2017.1313883.

Vraga, E. K. and Bode, L. (2020). Defining misinformation and understanding its bounded nature: Using expertise and evidence for describing misinformation. *Political Communication*, 37(1), pp.136–144.

Vraga, E. K. and Bode, L. (2022). Correcting what's true: Testing competing claims about health misinformation on social media. *American Behavioral Scientist*, 69(2). https://doi.org/10.1177/00027642221118252.

Vraga, E. K., Kim, S. C., and Cook, J. (2019). Testing logic-based and humor-based corrections for science, health, and political misinformation on social media. *Journal of Broadcasting & Electronic Media*, 63(3), pp.393–414.

Waddell, T. F. (2018a). This tweet brought to you by a journalist: How comment gatekeeping influences online news credibility. *Electronic News*, 12(4), pp.218–234. https://doi.org/10.1177/1931243117739946.

Waddell, T. F. (2018b). What does the crowd think? How online comments and popularity metrics affect news credibility and issue importance. *New Media & Society*, 20(8), pp.3068–3083. https://doi.org/10.1177/1461444817742905.

Waddell, T. F. (2020). The authentic (and angry) audience. *Digital Journalism*, 8, pp.249–266. https://doi.org/10.1080/21670811.2018.1490656.

Walter, N., Brooks, J. J., Saucier, C. J., and Suresh, S. (2021). Evaluating the impact of attempts to correct health misinformation on social media: A meta-analysis. *Health Communication*, 36(13), pp.1776–1784. https://doi.org/10.1080/10410236.2020.1794553.

Wang, B. and Zhuang, J. (2018). Rumor response, debunking response, and decision makings of misinformed Twitter users during disasters. *Natural Hazards*, 93, pp.1145–1162. https://doi.org/10.1007/s11069-018-3344-6.

Wang, Y. (2021). Debunking misinformation about genetically modified food safety on social media: Can heuristic cues mitigate biased assimilation? *Science Communication*, 43, pp. 460–485. https://doi.org/10.1177/10755470211022024.

Wang, Y. and Diakopoulos, N. (2022). highlighting high-quality content as a moderation strategy: the role of new york times picks in comment quality and engagement. *ACM Transactions on Social Computing*, 4(4). https://doi.org/10.1145/3484245.

Weeks, B. E., Ardèvol-Abreu, A., and Gil de Zúñiga, H. (2017). Online influence? Social media use, opinion leadership, and political persuasion. *International Journal of Public Opinion Research*, 29(2), pp.214–239.

Wike, R., Silver, L., Fetterolf, J., et al. (2022). Social media seen as mostly good for democracy across many nations, but US is a major outlier. *Pew Research Center*, 6.

Wineburg, S., Breakstone, J., McGrew, S., et al. (2022). Lateral reading on the open Internet: A district-wide field study in high school government classes. *Journal of Educational Psychology*, 114(5), p.893.

Wineburg, S. and McGrew, S. (2017). Lateral reading: Reading less and learning more when evaluating digital information. *SSRN*. https://doi.org/10.2139/ssrn.3048994.

Winter, S., Brückner, C., and Krämer, N. C. (2015). They came, they liked, they commented: Social influence on Facebook news channels. *Cyberpsychology, Behavior, and Social Networking*, 18, pp.431–436. https://doi.org/10.1089/cyber.2015.0005.

Wojcieszak, M., Thakur, A., Ferreira Gonçalves, J. F., Casas, A., Menchen-Trevino, E., and Boon, M. (2021). Can AI enhance people's support for online moderation and their openness to dissimilar political views? *Journal of Computer-Mediated Communication*, 26, pp.223–243. https://doi.org/10.1093/jcmc/zmab006.

Wojcik, S., Messing, S., Smith, A. W., et al. (2018). *Bots in the Twittersphere*. Pew Research Center. https://pewresearch.org/internet/wp-content/uploads/sites/9/2018/04/PI_2018.04.09_Twitter-Bots_FINAL.pdf.

Wood, T. and Porter, E. (2019). The elusive backfire effect: Mass attitudes' steadfast factual adherence. *Political Behaviour*, 41, pp.135–163.

Woodford, A. (2018). Expanding fact-checking to photos and videos. *Meta*. Available at https://about.fb.com/news/2018/09/expanding-fact-checking.

Yang, J., Barnidge, M., and Rojas, H. (2017). The politics of "unfriending": User filtration in response to political disagreement on social media. *Computers in Human Behavior*, 70, pp.22–29.

Zeng, H.-K., Lo, S.-Y., and Li, S.-C. S. (2024). Credibility of misinformation source moderates the effectiveness of corrective messages on social media. *Public Understanding of Science*, 33(5), pp.587–603. https://doi.org/10.1177/09636625231215979.

Zhang, Y., Guo, B., Ding, Y., et al. (2022). Investigation of the determinants for misinformation correction effectiveness on social media during COVID-19 pandemic. *Information Processing & Management*, 59, 102935. https://doi.org/10.1016/j.ipm.2022.102935.

Zhao, W. (2019). Misinformation correction across social media platforms. In *2019 International Conference on Computational Science and Computational Intelligence (CSCI)*, pp.1371–1376. https://doi.org/10.1109/CSCI49370.2019.00256.

Acknowledgments

Florian Stöckel and Jason Reifler acknowledge support from the British Academy (grant SRG20\200348). Jason Reifler would like to additionally acknowledge funding support from the European Research Council (ERC) under the European Union's Horizon 2020 research and innovation program (grant agreement No. 682758). We would like to thank Besir Ceka and Davidson College for their involvement in parts of the project and for generously allowing us to use the data we created collectively. We would also like to thank Chiara Ricchi and Jane Mitchell for their outstanding research assistance. We are very grateful for the thoughtful and constructive feedback provided by the two anonymous reviewers, which greatly improved our manuscript. The supportive guidance from the series editor, James Druckman, was invaluable, and we sincerely appreciate his recommendations and advice throughout the process. Florian is deeply thankful to Carolin for being in his life and for her unwavering support, and to Marie whose arrival has transformed their life in the most wonderful way. Ben thanks Julian, Beckett, and Ruby who are quick to correct him when he's wrong. Hannah would like to thank her family for their unconditional support and steady encouragement to pursue her dreams. Jason thanks his wife, Amy, for sharing this journey with him, and especially thanks Eleanor and Lila for being a constant reminder that there is good in this world and that the future is worth fighting for.

Cambridge Elements

Experimental Political Science

James N. Druckman
University of Rochester

James N. Druckman is the Martin Brewer Anderson Professor of Political Science at the University of Rochester. He served as an editor for the journals Political Psychology and Public Opinion Quarterly as well as the University of Chicago Press's series in American Politics. He currently is the co-Principal Investigator of Time-sharing Experiments for the Social Sciences (TESS) and sits on the boards of the American National Election Studies, the General Social Survey, and the Russell Sage Foundation. He previously served as President of the American Political Science Association section on Experimental Research and helped oversee the launching of the Journal of Experimental Political Science. He was co-editor of the Cambridge Handbook of Experimental Political Science and Advances in Experimental Political Science. He authored the book Experimental Thinking: A Primer on Social Science Experiments. He is a Fellow of the American Academy of Arts and Sciences and has published approximately 200 articles/book chapters on public opinion, political communication, campaigns, research methods, and other topics.

About the Series

There currently are few outlets for extended works on experimental methodology in political science. The new Experimental Political Science Cambridge Elements series features research on experimental approaches to a given substantive topic, and experimental methods by prominent and upcoming experts in the field.

Cambridge Elements

Experimental Political Science

Elements in the Series

Should You Stay Away from Strangers?: Experiments on the Political Consequences of Intergroup Contact
Ethan Busby

We Need to Talk: How Cross-Party Dialogue Reduces Affective Polarization
Matthew S. Levendusky and Dominik A. Stecula

Defection Denied: A Study of Civilian Support for Insurgency in Irregular War
David S. Siroky, Valery Dzutsati and Lenka Bustikova

Abstraction in Experimental Design: Testing the Tradeoffs
Ryan Brutger, Joshua D. Kertzer, Jonathan Renshon and Chagai M. Weiss

Examining Motivations in Interpersonal Communication Experiments
Elizabeth C. Connors, Matthew T. Pietryka and John Barry Ryan

Machine Learning for Experiments in the Social Sciences
Jon Green and Mark H. White II

Quality Control: Experiments on the Microfoundations of Retrospective Voting
Austin Ray Hart and J Scott Matthews

Inside the Radicalized Mind: The Neuropolitics of Terrorism and Violent Extremism
Tiffany Howard

Elitism versus Populism: Experiments on the Dual Threat to American Democracy
Curtis Bram

The Power of the Crowd: How the Public Can Both Spoil and Improve Social Media as a Source of Information
Florian Stöckel, Sabrina Stöckli, Benjamin A. Lyons, Hannah Kroker and Jason Reifler

A full series listing is available at: www.cambridge.org/EXPS

For EU product safety concerns, contact us at Calle de José Abascal, 56–1°,
28003 Madrid, Spain or eugpsr@cambridge.org.

www.ingramcontent.com/pod-product-compliance
Lightning Source LLC
LaVergne TN
LVHW011850060526
838200LV00054B/4259